BURIED GARDEN

Chris McCabe's work spans artforms and genres including poetry, fiction, non-fiction, drama and visual art. His work has been shortlisted for the Ted Hughes Award and the Republic of Consciousness Prize. His latest poetry collection, *The Triumph of Cancer*, is a Poetry Book Society Recommendation and he is the editor of several anthologies including *Poems from the Edge of Extinction: An Anthology of Poetry in Endangered Languages*. His first novel, *Dedalus*, is a sequel to *Ulysses*; his second, *Mud*, a version of the legend of Orpheus and Eurydice, set beneath Hampstead Heath. He works at the National Poetry Library in his role as the National Poetry Librarian.

ALSO BY CHRIS MCCABE

THE LOST POETS OF THE MAGNIFICENT SEVEN

In the Catacombs: A Summer Among the Dead Poets of West Norwood Cemetery (2014)

Cenotaph South: Mapping the Lost Poets of Nunhead Cemetery (2016)

The East Edge: Nightwalks with the Dead Poets of Tower Hamlets (2019)

NON-FICTION

Real South Bank (2016)

FICTION

Dedalus (2018)

Mud (2019)

POETRY

The Hutton Inquiry (2005)

Zeppelins (2008)

THE RESTRUCTURE (2012)

Speculatrix (2014)

The Triumph of Cancer (2018)

AS EDITOR

The New Concrete: Visual Poetry in the 21ˢᵗ Century, with Victoria Bean (2015)

Poems from the Edge of Extinction: An Anthology of Poetry in Endangered Languages (2019)

No, Love is Not Dead: An Anthology of Love Poetry from Around the World (2021)

Buried Garden

Lockdown with the Lost Poets

of Abney Park Cemetery

CHRIS MCCABE

Penned in the Margins

LONDON

PUBLISHED BY PENNED IN THE MARGINS
Toynbee Studios, 28 Commercial Street, London E1 6AB
www.pennedinthemargins.co.uk

First published in 2021

Printed in the United Kingdom by TJ Books of Cornwall

ISBN
978-1-908058-85-0

The author acknowledges the support of Arts Council England

CONTENTS

For my son, Pavel

Buried Garden
§
Lockdown with the Lost Poets of Abney Park Cemetery

My cousin said it was an amazing place. Not a bit like the ordinary London parks ... You go in through a gateway, and he said it was like finding yourself in another country. Such trees, that must have been brought from the end of the world: there were none like them in England ... deep hollows with streams running from the rocks; lawns all purple and gold with flowers, and golden lilies too, towering up into the trees, and mixing with the crimson of the flowers that hung from the boughs...

    Harliss did not fail with his response, 'I tell you there's no such place.'

ARTHUR MACHEN, 'N'

The Garden of the Egyptian Dead, 3150 BC

I am the poet of these grounds   I am the only one
I am the overseer of my garden   I am the only one
At my birth the four pillars were yet to rise   the city made them so
The seven gates of London are the protectors of lost poets travelling
The portal to the underworld gives access to the northwest passage
Anubis weighs your heart in the scales   he is Abney's
What was it that was here yesterday and is here still?
My body of work
Who was it who was not defeated by mundane lethargy   the daily
                                                        cull of grain?
I was not defeated
Who is the keeper of the book of things   which were or could be?
It is you my reader
Now enter

Entering the Abode of the Mortal Part of Man

TO STAND AT THE GATES of Abney Park Cemetery is to stare through a portal into the afterlife. Hundreds of people walk past here every day, missing the gateway. Four white columns rise from the high street, their capitals blackening where the stone meets the sky. This is Egyptian symbology: there are none of the Gothic touches you find at the entrances to the other Magnificent Seven, the great Victorian cemeteries encircling London. The Egyptian text, written on the inside lodges, translates as: ABODE OF THE MORTAL PART OF MAN.

Continuing my search for a great, lost poet in London's Magnificent Cemeteries, this is the fourth abode of the mortal part of man I have entered. South London brought me close, with the discovery of Menella Bute Smedley in West Norwood, and Walter Thornbury in the labyrinth of Nunhead. Frustrated by this proximity to success, I then crossed the Thames; what Tower Hamlets lacked in genius was filled with the unmissable life story of William 'Spring' Onions. That was a journey under the cover of nighttime, in a cemetery that never closes, but now I'm being led towards the dead by a different force: nature itself. Abney Park Cemetery is an unlikely London space, a former arboretum that still thrives amidst the smoke and thunder of Stoke Newington High Street. I've entered London's buried garden.

I am here today at the end of a lockdown winter, the weather yet to turn. I want to feel my way into this space, heading towards a spring spent walking above dead poets, with maps turning to roses in the hand, reading forgotten poems back to those who wrote them. After a landlocked year at home in Liverpool, a rip of possibility appeared in the shroud of the pandemic; I booked a train to be in this space that I've been thinking about so much. For the past decade, Liverpool has been my home city and London my city of work and imagination. Abney Park Cemetery is 31 acres in size, shaped like a distended liver, and is enclosed in a densely populated enclave of north-east London, on the path of the culverted Hackney Brook. Nestled between Dalston to the south and Tottenham to the north, the cemetery edges the path of Ermine Street, the Roman road from London to York.

For a long time, I've been obsessed with Arthur Machen's story 'N', in which three friends discuss the existence of a beautiful, transient landscape garden in Stoke Newington. The garden only appears to the few. It is a garden of both joy and terror, which quickly transitions from paradise to post-developed wasteland. As I continue my journey – or 'London Adventure', to use Machen's phrase – towards unearthing the dead poets of Abney Park, I am also starting to believe that the cemetery itself is the sublime lost garden of Stoke Newington.

Then one afternoon I fell asleep and had a dream about a visionary garden, made of liquid light. I wrote the dream down. That night I dreamt of another. I notice a pattern in the dreams as the characters – some real, others imagined – travail towards their own garden spaces.

The search for this garden might lead me to the poet I am looking for. This is a burial ground filled with visionaries, who died believing that a transformation – a Second Coming or a Resurrection – was imminent. In 1840, the minister overseeing the opening ceremony of the cemetery said: 'we know that when the figure of the Archangel shall loom on the distant sky, and the fiat shall be uttered, Arise ye dead! – it shall fall with startling – with vivifying energy on the dull cold ear of death'. Locked at home, I have been looking through the archives and discover that some of these visionaries were poets. The fact of Abney Park Cemetery being a garden open to everyone was written into its original constitution, a manifesto which distinguishes it from the rest of the Magnificent Seven:

> The object of the company is the establishment of a General Cemetery for the City of London and its north-eastern suburbs, which shall be open to all classes of the community, and to all denominations of Christians without restraint in forms.

When Abney Park Cemetery opened it contained over 2,500 varieties of trees and plants, with four acres laid aside as a rosarium – a pink sea of 1,000 specimens of rose. Visitors could also see quince trees, olive trees and laburnum. George Loddiges was commissioned as the landscape gardener and he included all the hardy plants from the pages of his journal, *The Botanical Cabinet* (1817-33), the drawings for which were taken from specimens grown in Hackney. This was a garden cemetery on a scale that had never been seen in London before. The earth itself was unique for its fertile sub-soils. George Collison, Abney's first secretary and registrar, documented the different kinds of earth found in the cemetery, from the 'fine sand' in the northern parts – that run for 20 feet below ground – to areas of 'fine vegetable mould' and London clay. 'This is blue of colour', he wrote, 'stiff in working, very plastic in nature, and almost free from stone'.

I'm walking over this hidden, blue earth, led by Machen's story into a garden landscape where poetry can be found: it appears in cryptic snatches on headstones everywhere I look. I return to Machen's description of Stoke Newington's lost garden, the one that is all around me:

> Before me, in place of the familial structures, there was disclosed a panorama of unearthly, of astounding beauty. In deep bells, bowered by overhanging trees, there bloomed flowers such as only dreams can show; such deep purples that yet seemed to glow like precious stones with a hidden but ever-present radiance.

Regeneration work is about to begin here. A sour cherry tree leans with limber fronds over a scaffold gate. Contracts are drawn and artist designs completed. The right lodge will extend into a Visitor Centre, with a Café and a reception for weddings. At one time, it was a maverick move to shoehorn married couples into a cemetery for samizdat photographs; now the death/desire paradigm is going viral.

Lockdown all around me: I made it here today against the odds. I have had so much more time to think over the past year, identifying the underlying pattern in my own life. A question has continued to occur to me, a tendril to the light: what will I choose to do with my body after death? As Reverend Barker wrote in his 1869 book *Abney Park*: 'nay, it is possible, if not probable, that thou thyself mayest ere long be separated from among the living, and thy narrow bed be found here'. I have been reading about how the body doesn't simply end with death; it too has its own afterlife, one that is related to the environment. The corporeal matter of the body is also a buried garden – one that can feed life in the earth – surviving in the remaining atoms.

Spring hangs on a precipice; new energy is on the verge of breaking through. I think of Machen's other great book, *The London Adventure* (1924), and am filled with the same optimism with which he sets about writing his work: 'I was to write a book about London ... But ... I was not going to begin writing it till the leaves were out on the trees, since the green leakage of the boughs made such a marvellous contrast with the grim greyness of the streets.' I walk past litter bins, a framed map of the grounds, appeals for volunteering. The rain of the past weeks has turned the boundary paths to gruel; the winter's gales have collapsed several trees. Fox dens have softened patches of earth so I watch my steps as I walk. This garden retains the darker side of Machen too; the oasis quickly shifts to eerie. Mushrooms can't be eaten here as they may be infused with arsenic – from the bodies of the Victorian dead – or lead from the coffins. A woman walks towards me, eyes foggy with lockdown fatigue, repeating the same words: 'horrible this is, horrible this is'. Stoke Newington High Street behind me: I've crossed the threshold.

One thing I have learned in my search for London's buried poets is that I will need to be quick, because summer foliage conceals headstones. Abney Park has grown wild since the description given by Barker in 1869:

> Its field of graves and intersecting paths are in that state of neat and decent order which should ever mark the resting-place of the dead. The visitor will be at once impressed by the evidences of the great care and attention which have been bestowed upon the general arrangement, and the daily efforts of the Company to keep church and tree, flower and shrub and monumental stone, in a state of perfection of beauty.

A decade later, the *Hackney and Kingsland Gazette* ran the following notice, indicating that the beginnings of the garden's dilapidation was under way:

ABNEY PARK CEMETERY

Notice to Freeholders

> Many gravestones, Tombs and Railings having fallen into decay and requiring immediate reparation, owners of Graves are requested to inspect their property in the Cemetery, and give directions as to necessary repairs.   By Order.
>
> Wm. BROWN, Secretary.

My search in the disintegrating garden has begun, a journey – in Machen's words – that deliberately 'shun[s] the familiar'. I've walked a circuit around the cemetery and am back at the gates. The Millennium has passed; the Second Coming did not happen: the portal remains open.

§

I receive a letter from my brother, handwritten on green paper. A tarot card falls out, the VIII Wands, the artwork showing hands falling from the sky – orchestrating a searing sun – and beneath them green hills, crosses wedged along a path:

> This card REALLY wanted you ... first it fell out of the deck while I was shuffling, and it appeared as the card I picked. It's the EIGHT OF WANDS – a speedy, strong, determined little bolt of creativity!

Have you had an idea about a little (or not so little) nature-based project recently? Perhaps something that uses your creative talent to connect you with nature?

The wands fly towards their target. The sun shines on their path. The hills are sharp and inviting. Holy crosses stand by the side of the path. Do any of the prompts in this card speak to you?

The paths are beginning to converge. I ask around people I know, those who might have an angle on Stoke Newington, to see if Machen's lost garden has appeared to them. The thing about Machen's story is that the garden appears to different people, in different spaces, and at different times. Poet Richard Price tells me about Alexandra Palace with its 'soft owl call – with the ghosts of its monkeys and deer'. Closer to Abney are his frequent walks through Ducketts Common, which – he says – 'is almost invisible because it just seems a scrap on the High Road between Harringay's Green Lanes and Wood Green High Road proper'. Could this be Machen's garden?

'A more likely Brig a' Doon garden', Richard says, 'is Russell Park, almost completely hidden in the heart of Noel Park estate. Like Ducketts Common, it has mature trees though much more bird life – it is alive with birdsong every time you visit. There are mini-allotment spaces on it.' He describes how a large tree, somehow weakened in the hot weather, fell across the path narrowly missing his son Rory, and Rory's mother, the poet Hannah Lowe. Richard's description of the landscape is compellingly Machenesque: 'As the New River winds about it also creates little patches of greenery that no-one can easily see – one near my place I incorporate into a morning walk. When I came to the block first to see if I wanted a flat there, I looked out the window of an unoccupied room high up and saw the blue green spark of a kingfisher shoot past below. It was one of the reasons, a kind of charm or sign, that I decided to move in'.

In Machen's 'N', the garden appears through windows – nature framed by a manmade portal. One day Glanville asks the Reverend to look out of the window; the Reverend does so, seeing only 'that which I had expected to see: a row or terrace of neatly designed residences'. It is then that Glanville says to him 'Look again', and the hidden garden appears: 'I might also say that my soul was ravished by the spectacle displayed before me. I was possessed by a degree of rapture and delight such as I had never experienced. A sense of beatitude pervaded my whole being'. This feeling of joy is quickly replaced with 'a swift revulsion of terror', and the Reverend runs from the house without saying a word. It might be that the garden is just too beautiful to behold for long, or that its association with madness makes it too dangerous to retain in the mind for any length of time. The key phrase in Machen's story is 'Look again', for without the volition to see – to look beyond the eyes – the garden will never appear in the first place.

I look again at my brother's letter: 'The sun shines on their path. The hills are sharp and inviting. Holy crosses stand by the side of the path.'

The garden exists for those who are ready to see it.

The Garden of Liquid Light, 1854

When she arrived at the garden, she lost her shadow.

The question remained as to whether she should continue or, as advised, return back to the city? Is it possible to move forward without a shadow? The gates to the garden were odd, a tapestry of still-growing briars which seemed to grow even as she looked at them. The only way through would be by force; there would be blood to pay for this. It was a price she *must* pay, because on the other side was the fountain, pumping out – not water – but liquid light. This was what she had come for.

She placed her compass and glass blade into her satchel, then threw it over the wall. Now she must go through – everything would be lost without her satchel. She pulled back the first of the briars, which nipped at her fingers. Back home there was a saying, 'red and green never to be seen unless there's something in between'. The in-between was her flesh, shredding as she squeezed through the trellis of thorns. An idea came to her, very strange, that nature was writing itself on to her body, in a language that she was yet to learn. What script had she willed herself to become? What syllabary was forming on her flesh? What new vowels were invented here, in The Garden of Liquid Light?

She lay in the dust of the garden, spent; then she crawled to her satchel and took the glass phial from inside, draining the last of the Aqua Corrective onto her tongue. She would be hydrated now for another week, but more importantly, she now had an empty phial to capture the liquid light. She looked down at the flesh of her torso, blood running like tears. History was about to change. Would it take only this, to transform her people from annihilation to victory?

She arrived at the fountain in the way a priest arrives at a font, holding the head of a blessed child.

She placed the phial beneath the liquid light ...

The Wild No Man's Land of the North

London, it was true, was unknowable, an unplumbed depth.
ARTHUR MACHEN, *THE LONDON ADVENTURE*

I'M LOST IN ABNEY PARK. The cemetery is an extension of Machen's labyrinthine north, with the allure of paradise or terror – one wrong turn leading to unalterable experience. This is what the fringes do: turn you inside out, expose you to a vernal light where the inner organs perform divination. 'The wild no man's land of the north', Machen describes it in 'N': 'Harliss … could not revisit them in talk with any glow of feeling … as if one were to discourse of Arctic Explorations, and lands of everlasting darkness.' I'm reminded of William Blake's description of his walks to the north of London, which he claimed made him feel ill – but still he kept returning, the pull to the fringes irresistible.

I look at my own tangled threads, written in my notebook; a mass of sketchy links. I am here to make a start, to take the first steps towards meeting Abney Park's lost poets.

The name 'Stoke Newington' derives from 'the new village in the wood', the wood in question being Middlesex Forest. The word 'stoc' is Saxon for 'wood' (or 'dwelling'). The village was first mentioned in the reign of Athelstan and the Domesday Book refers to it as 'Newtone', or Stoke Neweton: 'New Town'. The area was known for its horticulture, orchids, carnations, dahlias and ferns. Stoke Newington Church Street has been claimed as one of the oldest street names in London, first noted in the 14th century. The buried garden was always here, I think: its green spaces slowly replaced with brick.

'My earliest recollections of a school-life', Edgar Allan Poe writes in 'William Wilson' (1839), a story based on his school years in Stoke Newington, 'are connected with a large, rambling, Elizabethan house, in a misty-looking village of England, where were a vast number of gigantic and gnarled trees, and where all the houses were excessively ancient. In truth, it was a dream-like and spirit-soothing place, that venerable old town.' It took an outsider such as Poe to realise that the village of Stoke Newington could provide the perfect backdrop to the modern Gothic.

As Barker writes, even by 1869 this was 'a locality of considerable renown on account of the salubrity of the air, and its picturesque scenery'. But 'development' was already changing the area:

Before the subsoil began to be fashioned into bricks, and the builders commenced to eat up the land and transform trees into houses, it was the most picturesque of any suburb in London ... the gigantic railways and their termini, have compelled the inhabitants of the three-millioned city to find nests for themselves and their families in the suburbs, where the lark was once accustomed to soar aloft.

Barker talks of how 'the ear catches the echo' of this older history; Machen wiped the lens so that we could see it. In 1884 the *Times* wrote about the threat to Highgate Woods, highlighting Abney Park Cemetery as one of the remaining green spaces in northeast London: 'Stoke Newington is still kept fresh and pretty owing to the lovely grounds of Clissold-Park ... but how long these precious acres of wood and lawn may remain as they are is doubtful. When they in their turn have been built over, the miles of ground between Clerkenwell-green – now long since greenless – and Abney-park Cemetery will be represented on the map by one large blot of black.'

In a paradox as tightly constructed as any double helix, the creation of Abney Park Cemetery – as a 'depository for the dead' – has done more than any other development in the area to hold on to the old wood of Stoke Newington.

My thoughts come back to the Egyptians, who longed for

native trees, and perhaps developed the motif of the pillar (or *djed*) as a fetish for the natural features that they had to import from Syria, including the cedar. Is Anubis overlooking Abney Park? The Egyptian God of the afterlife and mummification, wolf-headed and lean-legged: a chimera, overseeing lost souls. Anubis is one of the oldest Egyptian Gods and has been found on many tombs from the First Dynasty of Egypt (ca. 3150 – 2890 BC). Change the letters and there's the near homophone: Abney / Anubis. Was the decision to add Egyptian script over the gates of the cemetery an invocation to this ancient death god, a coded message in the spirit of nonconformism, to connect with more ancient burial practices than those of 19th-century Britain? In ancient Egypt, Anubis had such a cult following that his image was added to the walls of tombs, perhaps as a deterrent to the wild dogs and jackals that would dig up dead bodies. In the way a vaccine contains elements of the virus itself, the Egyptians believed that a dog-god was the best way to deter wild dogs. The columns at Abney's gates might also represent the First Dynasty view of the afterlife; for these people, the afterworld existed above the earth, as a large flat surface, supported on four pillars.

Musician Will René tells me about visiting the cemetery with a friend from Devon, entering from the Stamford Hill side, striding with purpose towards Stoke Newington Church Street.

At least that's what they thought. Instead, they found themselves walking in circles, arriving – as all the lost do here – at the chapel. There is never anyone else around when you first discover the chapel – it is one of the buried garden's rules. Mass distorts chronology. London disappears.

Then Caroline Ritchie – Blakean researcher and poet – writes to me, asking to arrange a time to talk about William Blake. To think through his cartographical mapping of an alternative London. The real London. Via the sketchy portal of another lockdown Zoom, Caroline tells me how she lives just 15 minutes from the cemetery and will go walking there today, after our call. She mentions a poem she's written, about getting lost in the grounds: 'I don't know if that complete disorientation is in the vein of a visionary garden', she says. 'It was actually quite an intense experience, in a way. Normally I get lost a lot, but feeling so buried in the cemetery, where you can't see the streets at all – cars or anything – it was quite intense.' Here's someone else who has seen the visionary garden, and written it into evidence:

Inter

She walks to tangled edge
to fence like mental blank impassable

/ impossible

To stare a moment longer than polite
might be to find a foothold

Still she walks

in Abney labyrinth thick with feeling lost, gets lost
amid black poplar

(spread all over sky
makes small the airy way)

Dark maze won't knock it into

sense, bad place to come without a ball of string…
So reach for lighter find none ask stranger
for directions

Effect & cause dovetail,

sky & poplar, hedge & green: the right word
(always a power)

flickers somewhere in

between

Later, Caroline sends me two photographs of the same fallen angel, lying on the ground in Abney Park; the first was taken in October 2020, the second in January 2021. The earlier photo shows the angel newly fallen, in a bed of nettles, its stone surface still white and relatively undappled. The second photo shows the lockdown none of us saw from our homes; the angel's face has turned pea-green, a lichen beard forming around the mouth. The recesses of its stone skirt are black with moss, bacteria forming in the apertures of the toes. Someone has slightly moved the head, which is now broken from its torso. The angel has slept through it all.

Caroline's poem 'Inter' is a fragmented lyric – buckling under the linguistic stress of trapped energy and claustrophobia – which recounts a woman walking to the 'tangled edge' where a 'mental blank' takes place (in Machen's 'N', this is described as 'great perturbation and confusion of mind'). The poem solidifies another hunch I have about Abney Park, that it forces the 'I' into the third person. When you arrive at the chapel for the first time, there is a sense of seeing yourself from above. 'Still she walks', the poem goes, 'in Abney labyrinth thick with feeling lost'. Her description of black poplars 'spread all over the sky' is consistent with Machen's account of the lost garden; as Machen writes: 'Where I had seen valleys embowered in green leafage, waving gently in the sunshine and the summer breeze, there were now boughs bare and black, scarce showing so much as a single bud'. When the garden turns black, Machen's characters flee. Caroline, like me, remains, looking for 'the right word', for the 'effect & cause'. This is a 'bad place to come without a ball of string'.

Today I have threads, but no string. A host of random, unlinked names have been sent my way, or retrieved from historic newspaper archives. The account of a stone mason who keeled over mid-sentence, while pointing at a monument; a young woman who died a few weeks after her wedding and was interred in her bridal dress; the rumour that Cromwell's remains are buried in the grounds.

Abney attracts strangeness. On 23rd September 1848, the *Berkshire Chronicle* reported a burial here that could have come from one of Edgar Allan Poe's tales. It describes how the master of St Luke's workhouse – a man named as Bacon – had been found dead, washed up on the cost of Abergavenny. He was one of 178 who had died following the burning of the Ocean Monarch ship, after its disembarkation from Liverpool. It transpired that Bacon had left his wife and children to flee with the wife of the school master of the workhouse, to start a new life in America. What adds to the strangeness is that a few years earlier, Bacon had travelled throughout the United States, searching for the rate collector of St Luke's, who had stolen thousands of pounds of parish money. Bacon's body was identified by papers in his pockets and the clothes he was wearing.

There was also a case of premature burial here. In October 1885 the *Fife News* reported:

RESCUED FROM THE GRAVE.—On Monday week an infant, 3 months ... was seized with convulsions, which were supposed to have resulted in death. The little body was duly prepared for burial, and on Saturday last the internment took place at Abney Park Cemetery. While the coffin was being lowered a child's cry was heard, and as soon as the lowering had been completed a cry was again heard. Attention being thus drawn to the coffin, it was drawn up and the top unscrewed, when it was found that the little one was alive. The child was taken home, and is now in a fair way of recovery.

Abney Park fits the definition of 'eerie', as proposed by Mark Fisher: 'release from the mundane, this escape from the confines of what is ordinarily taken for reality'. I look at the open space in front of me, no one else around and there's no doubt that this space fits Fisher's definition. Detachment from the mundane pressures of the everyday. Disengagement from the city. False calm. London writer Andrew Gough found a pig's head here in 2009. There is an extant picture of Gough holding up the head with a stick, snout upturned to the chapel, its weathered skin caked with blood and dried loam.

These stories I'm discovering also fit with Fisher's definition of the 'weird': 'the weird is that which does not belong … the weird brings to the eerie something which ordinarily lies beyond it, and which cannot be reconciled with the "homely". The form that is perhaps most appropriate to the weird is montage.' I'm adopting the technique of montage as a method to take me closer to the weirdness of Abney Park. Newspaper clippings, lost poems, prose, dreamt fiction. When the Reverend Thomas sees the garden in 'N', it shifts from eerie to weird, becomes 'chimerical' and 'adumbrated', suggesting a place that is hinged *onto* London, that is unaccountable, impossible to assimilate: 'in place of familiar structures … a panorama of unearthly, of astounding beauty'.

I've just discovered Bridget Penney's writing about the cemetery, an ongoing series of blog posts, PDFs and drawings, interweaving walks amongst Abney's trees with connected images from Ovid. After one of her visits, she wrote: 'Trees, spiders and statues are all very much present in the "managed wilderness" of Abney Park today.' Form grows from landscape.

It was always raining at burials here. Pollock splashes on the hems of heavy black coats. Graveside services cut short, to a mere hour, against the tide of Victorian oratory. Close family filling in the hole – the sons away in Australia, not enough notice to make it back (the dead buried in two days) – their place at the grave occupied by a stadium of unnamed leisure watchers. Death as a pastime, closer than we could possibly know – even in a time of virus – but pushed back into its lacunae with song, prayer, pie and shawl. Attending a funeral was a reliable way to get your name in print, with journalists fleshing out obituaries with the details of those who attended. The ultimate vanity publishing.

The burial of Mrs Booth, the wife of General Booth, captures this Victorian pastime well. 'She passed in darkness out of sight', the *Liverpool Mercury* reported in 1890, a passage no doubt scripted by one the many frustrated writers, cutting their teeth in the epic jaws of literary ambition. 'The fog destroyed the impressiveness of the procession and the ceremony ... and at the same time lent to it such mystery which does not usually attend such functions'. It was clearly the journalist's first burial in Abney Park. Two years later, in an episode that could have been written by Lewis Carroll, a woman fittingly called Mrs Patience used her prayer book to whack off the hat of a mourner. 'The wind was cold and the rain icy', London's *Daily Telegraph & Courier* reported, which was why the offending Mr Barstow had only lifted his hat, rather than take it off altogether.

Today, the Covid-19 pandemic has reset the rules on burial practices. Funerals restricted to 30 people, families streaming through the white spittle of lagging screens. Glitching Android. In Mexico, the Day of the Dead is cancelled, the national night for remembrance and carnival embargoed until further notice. Bodies in hospital corridors, pale wrists tagged with green bands. Grief without closure. Hospices closed, entrances hazard taped. The dead as a disenfranchised class, a picket line of the forgotten. News alert: a ship called the Evergreen blocks the Panama Canal. A metaphor for stalled grief. First you can't hug, then there's no one to hug. Time out of flow.

Earlier this week I had another garden dream; this time I was trapped in a miniature Japanese garden, navigating my way through the foliage with a journey across the surface of a leaf taking a decade. Was it a metaphor for my journeys through the Magnificent Seven or a subconscious response to lockdown?

Ahead of me, two men are scoping the closed cemetery toilets, hoping for access. 'Anyone in there?' one asks. Nothing. Then they follow me into the grounds, beer cans in hand. 'See those tree stumps', one explains to the other, 'they want to grind them into the ground'. He's wearing a black cape and a hat, knows every tree that's ever been planted here; blackout visions of the rosarium. A documenter of past changes, standing on the verge of mass change in Abney Park.

I look at my notebook and start my journey towards meeting the dead poets with the name 'John Dryden' (birth date unknown). He is not the well-known Augustan poet, but a namesake, who died at the age of 31. There is no evidence that Abney's Dryden ever wrote poetry, though his headstone, placed here in 1892, comes close: 'His sun is gone down while it was yet day'.

The next name in my notebook is William Ellis (1794-1872), who married a poet, Sarah Stickney (later Ellis, 1799-1872). She is buried in rural Cambridgeshire. William died of a cold, in 1872, and Sarah followed a week later. He is buried near to the centre of the cemetery, in a hip tomb – a rectangular box, laid flat on the floor – aligned with the chapel. Then there is a Mrs Catherine Steer (-1879), who as a child had been sat on Coleridge's knee. It is an image heaving with symbolism, suggesting something of the poetic legacy handed from the Romantics to the Victorians. I picture the child in starched black clothes, as Coleridge stares into empty space, envisioning the miraculous. Her funeral was overseen by the poet-Reverend, Edwin Paxton Hood, who I note as a name to look in to later. Might he be the poet I'm looking for?

I stop at the chapel and read the graffiti, inside and out. Can I take the graffiti as poetry? A graffito in the cemetery is different than a scrawled tag on the shutters of an off-licence. It is writing for the viewing of the dead. In art theory, 'graffiti' is usually defined as a scratch in a surface that reveals a further layer underneath. In the context of the cemetery, graffiti could be the arising thoughts of the dead, swimming into focus. Asemic doodles written in the hinge between life and death.

The history of graffiti is closely connected to the development of burial rites and the cult of death. The term 'graffiti' once referred to the vandalised graphics that were found on the walls of sepulchral ruins, such as the catacombs at Pompeii and Paris. These were often declarations of love, or the textual eviscerations of those who'd been spurned by a lover. Paul Koudounaris, in *The Empire of Death: A Cultural History of Ossuaries and Charnel Houses*, describes the 'rampant graffiti' that has taken place in the ossuary chapel in Évora: 'The majority of the skulls have at some point been marked with people's names in pencil or pen, sometimes carved directly into the bone. Even the head of the mummified man, some three metres above the floor, was somehow marked by a graffiti tag.' The prevalence of graffiti in places of death shows a deep human urge in the living to leave a mark, a life-affirming gesture that resists our own mortality:

'if the charnel house engages visitors in a dialogue with death', Koudounaris argues, 'perhaps these marks are part of the ongoing conversation'.

One of the graffitos here reads 'JOY-RIDES'. A crow walks towards me, bottom-weighted, defying its Nevermore. A jogger paces past, spits, heading straight towards the Isaac Watts monument. A woman approaches with a Labrador, talking – I expect to see a phone in her hand, but she's talking to the dog: 'Well she would, she would say that wouldn't she?' A woodpigeon fires the rifles of its wings. A mother walks with a toddler. He is wearing a helmet and asking 'You mean the green alien?' An inexplicable smell of tobacco rises from the undergrowth.

I flick through the catalogue of interns listed in Paul Joyce's *Guide to Abney Park Cemetery*, imagining each of them in life. Now it's our turn.

The Garden of Zen, 1640

I spent most of my life lost in the Zen garden of Daisen-in.

My early years were spent wandering the miniature river, as it forked into branches, symbolic of the follies of youth. It was only when I'd passed through this first phase that I realised that the landscape was sculpted into a letter L.

The screen paintings that faced me were so real, it was impossible to know whether I was at the frontier of a new world or had been subjected to the constraints of my own imagination. So real was the artist's vision. I scratched a huge letter 'I' into the canvas, at last proving to myself that I could go past the illusion.

My middle age was spent in a garden of rocks, overlooking the Middle Ocean. I was soon physically subjected to these rocks, which represented the obstacles of mid-life. I was catapulted by boat into the sea. For five years I sailed along the first branch of a letter 'F', before realising it was the longer, upper branch of the letter that would gift me my escape.

My destiny was the three mountains beyond the ocean. The search for the wisdom of an epic vowel, an upturned E. This final destination would bring peace and serenity. A turtle passed me by, swimming against the tide, symbolic of the world that should never be met with force.

Now through wisdom my transformation to human size could be achieved. I would soon look back on my life as a man would, who looks down upon an ornate wormery. The pathways of my efforts were etched forever into the garden. I read the word LIFE as I plucked the leaf it had taken me ten years to travel across.

Hazard Taping the Dead

—— GEORGE & ISABELLA VARLEY BANKS

I have burnt my fingers to the bone again and again in the last forty years and I dread the fire of literature.
ARTHUR MACHEN, *THE LONDON ADVENTURE*

PEOPLE BREAK OUT OF LOCKDOWN with sudden jets of purpose; striding for trains that jar, bolt, catch the engine and move – away from the cramp of basement desks. This is how my commute from Liverpool should always be: whole tables isolated for a single person, no interference for ticket checks; space, quiet, calm. Cows stare at the train as it passes, bemused by the low head count. I fall asleep and wake at Euston. London. The landscape of my pandemic dreaming is suddenly available to touch.

Arthur Machen wrote: 'All the wonders lie within a stone's throw of King's Cross Station'. Contractors have used the cover of lockdown to rewrite London's streets. The Slug and Lettuce outside Euston station has gone, eaten by the caterpillar of development. I jump on the bus towards Abney Park, with two poets to seek out and discover: the married couple Isabella Varley Banks (1821-1897) and George Linnaeus Banks (1821-1881). The bus moves at speed, cutting like a red blade through grey sponge. The journey that took an hour in pre-pandemic pandemonium takes 20 minutes.

Slate-grey pavements glisten in the rain. Commuters stall through collective brainfog. I pass Cumming Street and can't help thinking of Dominic, the farce of the first lockdown; today the city feels like a test drive in order to prove it is fit to travel through. Islington Green. Angel. A man with a pink hat and an eyepatch stands – still as a heron – knowing something I don't.

Scaffolds mark changing territory. Essex Road Station. Northchurch Road. London eerie: a lack where there should be something: people. There are stragglers, but none of the usual great attrition – the shared drive to meet – to make, to capture and to triumph.

Then panic on the bus. A missed stop becomes a catastrophe as a man reaches for the cap over the emergency exit button, tugging the roof for freedom. 'My stop!', he shouts, 'I've missed my fucking stop!' Acidic exchanges with the driver. Doors open with the snort of a bull. Then a heavy clattering as the man jumps and hits the pavement. High pitched cursing. Lifeblood. The bus moves on towards the cemetery.

I was looking for my first Abney poet and found two. Married. I look into Isabella Varley Banks first; in fact, Victorian press gave her more pages than her husband. She was born in Manchester and died in Hackney. Unknown to her, her words were later used by Factory Records owner Tony Wilson for the epitaph on his headstone; he took the words, cut the punctuation and lineated:

Mutability is the epitaph of worlds
Change alone is changeless
People drop out of the history of a life as of a land
though their work or their influence remains.

Reading about Banks and Wilson may have influenced my latest garden dream. Although Wilson never signed Mark E. Smith and The Fall, he did put them on his television show. My dream revealed that M.E.S. knew the exact details of a visionary garden but he had recorded the information onto a tape device which had ended up at the bottom of the sea.

I pass through the Egyptian gates, heading straight for the north of the cemetery where the Banks are buried.

Given the pressures of Banks' life, it is incredible that she got anything down on paper at all. Her husband was restless, forcing the family frequently to relocate and becoming increasingly jaded by his own lack of fame as writer. He was also an alcoholic, and bad with money. The couple had eight children, but only three of them survived into adulthood. Experiencing a nervous breakdown, ailing health and the unexpected death of her mother, Banks kept the family afloat by writing for six hours straight in the early mornings. It was the self-dug bunker that allowed her to create; she produced 12 novels, three volumes of short stories and three collections of poetry.

So much is known about Banks, and so much of her work still in print, but the headstone might not be so easy to find. I have come with ballast to this headwind, a contact for one of Abney's Trust Coordinators, who has provided some directions to the grave. The location has been marked for me with hazard tape, strips of red and white gaffer, spiralling to pink in the breeze. The problem is finding the hazard tape. Stumbling on the broken path of Little Elm Walk, I send my contact a text to ask for help, and she responds straight away, a personal GPS in this urban wilderness:

> go back down 2—2.5 meters there should be an 'obvious' ie relatively clear path, about 5 rows in is a big fallen tree. The grave is kind of against the trunk and there is a hazard tape near it but on the right

> of it, on ivy. Grave is illegible. Take that path in and follow veering
> right near fallen tree – path gets less obvious in places – as they all do!

I'm reaching the centre of the garden, where paths begin to disappear. All paths end somewhere, and not always at the feet of a dead poet.

Sometimes the internet provides a gauge to the level at which a writer is still read today. There is an audio version of Banks' novel *The Manchester Man* on YouTube, freely available, read in the Mancunian accent of Phil Benson. Ten of Banks' books are listed on goodreads.com, with *The Manchester Man* being far the most popular (98 ratings at 4.01 stars – many contemporary novelists would covet this). Amongst the unrated books is *Ripples and Breakers: A Volume of Verse* (1893).

There are two individual poems on poemhunter.com, a site which includes a 'popularity' graph, which in Banks' cases dips from the year 2017, showing the poems haven't been read on that site for four years. Her poem 'Bridal Robes' is included amongst them, and although it is a poem which largely conforms to the tropes of chastity prevalent at the time, there are two things I like in it. The first is the form, with the syllables of each stanza increasing towards the middle, then decreasing again in its final line. It gives a sense of weaving, which chimes with the theme of the robes, and also of how life is pieced together from experience. The final line, written in monosyllables, reinforces death's finality:

> And only wife who kept
> As spotless her life as her dress,
> Be honoured to wear her bridal gown,
> Be honoured to wear her bridal crown,
> When Death should her pale lips press.

Ivy Leaves (1844) was written when Banks was just 23 years old; many of the poems are laden with fatigued expressions, such as 'Hush', 'o'er', 'Ah, me' (echoes of Milton) and lines written with a forced omniscience: 'the solemn stillness of the sleeper's trance' ('The White World'). This long, descriptive poem, about the physical state of a dying man, does have a notable moment, when he utters his final words: '"I've been" – a pause – "I've been to the White World"'. This foreshadows Machen's story 'The White People', written 50 years later, which contains a text from the perspective of a 16-year-old girl, describing strange events in the forest – seeing 'the white lady', leaving a doll made of clay under some bushes – until it is later revealed that the girl had died, her body found next to a pagan site. Banks' poem also invites us into the realm of the weird:

White world! hiding thy mysteries beneath
That flimsy-textured veil – Mortality,
Wast thou in truth revealed to the "mind's eye"
Of this sleep-fettered man, in dreamy semblance –
In visions that appeared reality?
Or had the soul...

                been disrobed
And led by guides angelic to the gates

The poems in *Ivy Leaves* are fixated with the body in its moment of dying, the terrain that John Henry Newman would explore with some majesty in *The Dream of Gerontius* (1865). In a similar way to Newman, Banks draws on Dante for her imagery: 'The fiery thirst that dries and crisps his tongue / Till his breath burns like flame!' ('The Funeral Bell'). These poems are dream visions of men about to die, capturing landscapes that the person will never visit, at other times revelling in the grotesque, such as 'a puny dwarf' that visits a usurer in his final hours ('Helon'). Banks is drawn to the reality of the physical body, sometimes working from newspapers sources, developing her poems with an eye for social realities. It transpires that the dying man in 'Helon' is a slave owner in Africa, his funeral rites left to a slave called Richard who 'resigns / The body of his best-loved friend ... / to its lonely Afric grave'. There are problems with Banks' vision, not least the resolution that an African slave – given an English name – should feel so much for this 'master'.

The path is behind me now, in front of me a fallen ash; purple fungi is attached to the trunk, growing – destined to become its own future species. The fungus itself is being eaten by something else. It's been that kind of year. I duck under the branch, staring at the fungus as I go under; I swear that it winks at me.

Although Banks's poems are framed by Christian theology, she also leaves space for the strange and unknown. In other poems, there are moments of acute observations, and striking imagery: 'Thou art too young for the grave / Pleasure is launching her bark for thee' ('Spirit of Earth'). She is at her best when she is not only in full flight with the dying body she is animating, but when she is also pushing the language *within* each line, so that poetic events occur on the micro level: 'Flitting athwart my visionary brain / As lights electric 'cross an arctic sky' ('Dream of an Enthusiast'). What impresses most in Banks's poems is the free reign of the imagination; she fully commits to her visions for ten pages or more, writing with an ability to keep the reader turning pages. It is easy to see why she moved towards fiction – here is a writer who wants to tell stories. Banks seems to have pushed the form of her poems as far as she could, becoming more absorbed in the stories she had to tell rather that the sustained phonetic explosions that poetry – even narrative poetry – relies on.

Banks' poems are invocations of place, and I wonder if her description of a cemetery in her poem 'The Funeral Bell' draws on experiences of visiting Abney Park:

> Here rested the remains of one who died
> In the first blush of childhood; – in one nook
> Reposed a village patriarch; and near
> Lay, side by side, two marble slabs, that told
> A tale of hapless love, – a watery grave
> The lover's …
>   and a modest tomb
> Erected by his flock, sets forth the worth
> Of a respected pastor.

Here we have the mention of a village, marble slabs, and 'a watery grave', which may be the Hackney Brook.

There is only one overseer in Abney: nature itself. The headstones buckle and totter under its pressure; some find themselves adopted in the branches of trees. It is true that writers are never in complete control of the destiny of their work, but in death, all control is relinquished. The body becomes bacterial matter.

Banks' poetry, unlike so many hundreds of Victorians, remains in print, available to buy in British Library editions – an afterlife secured. One of her characters says:

"I have touched the lyre's responsive string,
        Yet never dreamed of fame,
And my fancy's wild embodyings
        Have seldom settled aim;
            Yet have my lays
            Aye met with praise,
        And spread afar my name."

('The Gift of Song')

We do not know if Isabella Banks ever dreamed of fame, but her imaginative poems have spread her name as a writer and been met with praise.

George Banks' preface to *Spring Gatherings* (1845) is unsparing in its commitment to authorial 'success': 'My task is ended. I have wound into a wreath the wild flowers of my fancy – and all that now remains for the Author of "Spring Gatherings" to do, is to appear before that tribunal; which awaits every candidate for literary honours'.

Poetic reputation may be formed of many factors, but it is never overseen by a tribunal. Influence relies on a more amorphous process, gaining one reader at a time. Skill, graft – and sometimes chance – govern the poet's course. A poet can control the writing of the work itself, but seldom its reception.

Banks was born in Birmingham in 1821 to a nature-loving family; his father was a horticulturist. Banks' maternal grandfather was descended from Richard Penderel, who had helped King Charles II to hide in the oak tree at Boscobel. The grandfather, Joseph Hill, was a Wesleyan, and George's father hoped that his son would become a preacher for the same sect. Young George, however, was a dilettante, trying out careers as a metal engraver and a cabinet-maker, but also studying literature, realising that he was a good debater and public speaker. His early poetry developed into prose, and his contributions to journals such as *Hood's Magazine* (edited by Tom Hood, whom I wrote about in *Cenotaph South*), led to a career in journalism.

The trees bend in the wind and a male blackbird stops, looks, then stutters back to the undergrowth – looking for the female.

Banks also contributed to the London writing of his day, editing a 'miscellany' called *The Finger-post Guide to London* (1862), a kind of Victorian Wiki containing oddities ranging from 'that portion of ancient and modern London traversed by the Royal pageants' to a full list of cab prices itemised by location. We're so used to tapping a screen, GPS accessing our location, inciting algorithms to do everything for us; the Victorian approach was more tactile. In *The Finger-Post Guide*, the reader works crossways through a matrix of locations to find the detailed price for their planned journey. I try at random: Brixton rise (vertical axis) to Haymarket Lower end (horizontal axis): two shillings and six d, or £7.80 in today's money.

George Banks' first book of poems, *Blossoms of Poesy*, was published in 1841, three years before Isabella's. He followed this with *Lays for the Times* (1845) and *Spring Gatherings* (1845). The influence of his nature-loving father transcended to the son. It strikes me that George's interest in public speaking aligned itself with his verse – leading to a rhetorical poetry, that would be set to music by others.

He also began to write for the stage, writing a farce called *Tiger in Arms*, which was performed in 1842, and a drama called *The Swiss Father*, which was performed in Liverpool in 1846. He wrote a play for the black actor Ira Aldridge called *Ira, the Slave King*. Mixing in literary circles, it was on an evening in Manchester when he was introduced to Isabella, who had become known for *Ivy Leaves*. In conversations about poetry their married life began, ending somewhere along this path – but where? In front of me is a dense thicket of bramble and creeping ivy. I check the ground as I walk. A grey feather. A slug, gorging on a dog dropping. Abney's garden recycles.

It becomes clear that poetry, for George, was something kept running in the background of his life. He took on demanding editorships at the *Birmingham Mercury*, the *Dublin Daily Express*, the *Durham Chronicle* and the *Brighton Excursionist*. There are examples of poets whose work as journalists has strengthened their poetry – Barry MacSweeney and the American, Kenneth Fearing – but George made the mistake of responding too quickly to ephemeral stories, drastically reducing the shelf life of the poetic work.

Banks' better work is that which bypassed the immediacy of the news:

> And Nature, aroused from her pillow of snow,
> Whence the ice-torrent streamed in a deluge below,
> To a freshness of being enkindled, at once
> Leaps forth with a joyous response –
> With an instinct of beauty, essaying to sing
> The glory and praise of the life-giving spring.

> ('Spring')

The conceit employed here is that spring is like a waking animal, though the poem stalls through the verbosity and mid-line awkwardness of the language itself: 'a freshness of being enkindled'. What about 'fresh enkindling'? It is impossible not to compare this with Gerard Manley Hopkins's poem of the same title, in which words are fused together to create new potentialities of meaning, linguistic events that explode mid-line, always moving to an ever-changing metrical beat: 'Have, get, before it cloy, / Before it cloud'. As with so much Victorian poetry, Banks is held back by the imagined majesty of poetic voice – the rhetorical poise expected of an 'author'. Unknown poets have everything to gain by pushing to develop their own style as there is no readership to lose; it is best to write for one reader, directly, intimately – risking all on personal style. If that doesn't work out, at least the work will have pushed into new terrain.

I have entered new terrain myself, crossing the large but rugged landscape to the east of the Little Elm Walk. I look again at an object: what I thought was a skull is a fractal of polystyrene. A head composed of a crash helmet is a suitable image for a lockdown year.

Has Banks been speedily forgotten? The most well-known of his works is the poem 'What I Live For'; it was quoted by orators in his lifetime and still has a life online today. YouTube shows a woman breathing life into the verses, next to a stream in Wyoming:

I live for those who love me,
  Whose hearts are kind and true,
For heaven that smiles above me,
  And awaits my spirit too;
For the cause that lacks assistance,
For the wrong that needs resistance,
For the future in the distance,
  And the good that I can do.

Readers connect with the poem's sentiment, rather than for any detailed appraisal of its techniques; but what poet wouldn't want their words read by a new generation, born 150 years after their poem was written? It might have been enough to assuage George's jadedness. It is hard to imagine, standing in this untended corner of the cemetery, but Banks' work has travelled through time.

I've walked off the path, into the rutted section described by my contact. It is George Banks the nature lover that I connect with most, standing here, as a robin lands on a headstone; head left, right: working me out. There is something about reading the work of forgotten poets that stirs this gladness to be alive, in the body, in this moment: 'The short lived insect, borne on summer's wing', Banks wrote.

The husband and wife lie together in Abney earth, buried

somewhere here, on the Little Elm Walk. 'And "six feet of earth" be the conquest of Time', George Banks wrote, with prophetic certainty.

I take five steps further into the undergrowth and there it is: their headstone. At the long end of a short text message and a path I've left behind. The memorial has been eroded by time: text dissolving to silt. All that remains is a Celtic symbol at the top centre of the stone, unreadable due to the moss that has evened out its apertures.

§

As I walk out from the cemetery, my first real poets found, I think of Isabella Banks' poem 'Bridal Robes'. This poem connects with a true story about a burial in Abney Park, reported in the *Suffolk and Essex Free Press* on 21st August 1912. The headline ran 'Singular Funeral at Hoxton'. The story recounts how a 23-year-old bride, Florence E. Ridel, was buried wearing the wedding dress that she had been married in a few months before. She had died while rearranging furniture in her new home in Islington, lifting a dressing table alone – with all its contents inside – which caused a blood vessel to burst. Her condition deteriorated until she was brought home to die. What happened next was even stranger; the father laid out his dead daughter in his office, wearing her wedding clothes. He arranged around her the same orange blossoms and bouquet she had on her wedding day. 'Her bridal dress was of white satin, and this, with her white shoes, white stockings, and white veil, were all placed in the coffin.' Thousands of people came to the funeral, excited by the spectacle. The traffic was held up around the cemetery. The bride was late for her own funeral.

The father's logic was that the sight of the dress in the future would be too upsetting to see, so he wanted it out of view, below ground, with his daughter's remains. Her brothers commissioned a huge cross to be made from lilies, and 'there was an abundance of lilies-of-the-valley – the pet flower of the deceased girl'. I picture these as the rose varietal, and the lilies as Tango Lilies, their purple in synch with Machen's account of Stoke Newington's hidden oasis.

The more I think about it, the more I realise that what initially seems strange in this story might conform to the rules of ritual. The story has echoes of James George Frazer's descriptions of 'the Law of Contact or Contagion', described in *The Golden Bough*: 'Things which have once been in contact with each other continue to act on each other at distance after the physical contact has been severed'. Frazer also writes of 'the Law of Similarity', in which 'like produces like' (he uses the example of the husband of a pregnant wife rubbing his stomach to help bring on the birth);

for the staging of death as a wedding perhaps contains hope that death can match the happiness of the bride's wedding day. The coffin being made of the same mahogany as the chest that killed her isn't chance, as the journalist describes, but a psychological feint to transfer the cause of death below ground. As Frazer points out, there are ancient customs focused on aligning the things we touch, that contain an intuition that life and death can be transferred through contact. Amongst the 56 mourners at her graveside, many of them had been at her wedding: 'The fourteen wedding broughams were used', the report continues, 'with the footmen and coachmen who attended the wedding guests at church'. And here she lies, the buried garden of her future joys – perhaps children – lost inside the remains of her dead body.

I don't know what words were said at Florence's funeral, but I do know that Isabella Varley Banks' poem would have worked just fine:

And not 'till Death should call
The tried wife to his bridal bed,
Should that well-saved robe again be worn,
Or the orange-wreath again adorn,
That auburn or snow-white head.

The Garden of the Haçienda, 1983

What happened to the tape recorder? What happened to all the tape recorders, the world was built with them once: speaking bricks, capturing the dreams of every creative child?

But the answer we need could still be out there, trapped inside one specific unit. Mark E. Smith spoke into it, at the Haçienda club, in 1983. It surfaced from nowhere, as if out of his back pocket – but it was too big for his back pocket. He held the unit up to his face, speaking into its base; maybe even into the back of it. Then in the green room, after the show, Smith continued talking into the device, a demonic psycho-ramble that lasted an hour. It was the only true depiction of the lost garden, in which all of its seven gods were described.

The sea swims with reels of magnetic tape, silverfish unravelling the voices of the dead, speech unspooling like hatched eels – spawning phonemes – writing the future epic that will give us the answer to everything.

At this precise point on the sea floor, the debris field of broken machines hatch. All recorded words transform into the objects they name. On this, our deep-sea roving submersible, Lud III, we aim to find the objects materialised from Smith's words. In this way, we will reveal at last the long sought-for garden.

Millennial Angst & Antichrist

—— REVEREND DR HIBBERT NEWTON

For the beginning of my series I remember that I went back a good many years to the time when London began to call to me. I often speculate now in these later days as to how it would have been with me if this call had never come.

ARTHUR MACHEN, *FAR OFF THINGS*

THE LIFE OF THE REVEREND Hibbert Newton (1817-1892) spanned almost the entirety of Queen Victoria's reign, was followed with silence, and is now resurrected with a stark Wiki entry: 'poet and ... early proponent of British Israelism'. I have heard suggestions that the poets buried in Abney had a fixation with the Second Coming, and Newton confirms this. A year into the pandemic, I could do with one. It almost feels like a resurrection to have travelled the 200 miles to be here, in early April, with the winter refusing to throw in the shroud. Hibbert Newton is said to be buried near Abney's chapel, which gives me an excuse to circle it; to try and make sense of its Gothic – and parallactic – design.

Abney Park's chapel draws mass. It is like a drawing by Dutch artist M.C. Escher, the Dutch creator of impossible architectural constructions. Tessellation as pyscho-geometry: pathways to nowhere. Its gables are doubled – seem to replicate – so they look out two ways at once. Games of scale; finials reaching for the sky; stylus in the clouds. Stone blossoms. A tiny hut is positioned at the base of the building – a kiosk from which an eager apprentice could preach? Ivy creeps up the side, climbing between the gaps in the brick.

Newton studied divinity at Trinity College, Dublin and was ordained in 1847. In 1867 he became the vicar of St Michael's, Southwark, a position he kept until his death. His burial is something of an anomaly here, being a member of the Church of England.

A father and son stop and point at the chapel, the dad explaining how there was a space at the top where the funeral service could be watched. The boy, in Nike, reads aloud from an information board: 'The chapel is the oldest surviving non-denominational chapel in Europe'. I check my map to see if I'm on the right track to Newton, and when I turn, they have slipped away, pulled into the maelstrom of geometric bricks.

The campaign for British Israelism has its roots in the 16th century and became widespread in the 19th, following the publication of John Wilson's *Our Israelitish Origin* (1840). Newton was passionate about furthering this cause, with the *South London Chronicle* of 24th April 1880 announcing one of his events:

NOTES ON THE ENEMY

In a report of a great meeting in London of Ritualists and Liberationists, to elect fit Representatives for Parliament; with a Strain for Anglo-Israel in the Holy Land. By the Rev. Hibbert Newton, B.A., Vicar of St Michael's, Southwark.

According to the records of the British Library, Newton's first poetry publication – *The Vale of Tempe* – was published in 1830, which would have made him just 13. Bibliographic slip. The place of publication is Dublin, which concurs with the known facts of Newton's upbringing; a footnote to a poem elucidates the confusion: 'Composed during the Author's undergraduate course.' He would have been a young man then, with a drive towards illuminating history through his spiritual conviction: 'The events of this poem are supposed to take place about the middle of the third century, when the Goths repeatedly invaded Greece; the Emperor Decius lost his life in opposing them, and the Emperor

Gallienus with difficulty bargained their retreat'. The Vale of Tempe is a gorge in Thessaly, Greece, historically celebrated for its beauty and the ancient belief that it was frequented by Apollo and the Muses. Newton envisions a Second Coming to this time and place:

> As if the hand of Providence at last
> Came visible to bless what it began.

Here is a poet with a vision, laying down his version of a past Resurrection. On the level of the poetic line, there are moments of awkwardness, for example when Newton describes the 'earthly Paradise that smiles around'. This image is too abstract to work, it glides across the reader's mind, for whatever Paradise is, it does not smile. If Newton aims to anthropomorphise nature, he should commit to it fully, detailing every aspect of the vision. There are flashes of this, for example when he describes Mount Olympus as 'a giant form, / His forehead rears, hoar with eternal frost / Beneath him rolling views the thunder-storm, / And shrouds his head in low'ring vapour lost'. There is something of William Blake's descriptions of The Giant Albion in *Jerusalem*, but there is none of the cinematic jump-cuts, and sustained, deep imagery that we see in Blake – Newton's work soon slips back into vagaries.

Nature is never vague. As I walk, circling the chapel, a fledgling sparrow lands on the headstone before me, its head thick as a thumb, and stares at me, singing. Its chest heaves like a tarpaulin in a gale; its present need – these forages of never-ending winter – is everything. The bird looks up at the chapel, which has also shown its resilience, surviving the bombing of the cemetery in World War Two. It was built to be prominent – a magnetised needle in a sea of stone filings – but also to be functional; as George Collison writes: 'the spire should rise over the place where the bier would be deposited, and still be in the centre of the composition though out of the line of the road, and that the entrance should be by a porch under which processions should drive to set down under shelter from the weather, and free from the obtrusion of the curious'. The sparrow – curious – flits and makes for the spire.

As the poem goes on, Newton's praise for Jesus begins to dominate over poetic dexterity, the texture drowned in the message, though there are also encouraging levels of controlled musicality:

> He came, thine equal co-eternal Son,
> Unspar'd, and to the bitter cross was bound.

There is a further eccentricity to the work: Newton's footnotes for the 'critics'. While it is an obvious psychological impulse to close off potential critique before it can gain traction, there is no space in poetry for footnotes explaining what the poetry – in itself – should be doing: 'To understand this line, we must picture ourselves, that as the sun is falling behind the mountain, his rays gradually ascend towards the projections on its side, and when he is completely hidden those rays vanish'.

Newton calls the second half of his book 'Minor Poems', the inference being that 'The Vale of Tempe' is the 'Major' one. Poets are rarely the most reliable readers of their own work, and Newton's best poems actually appear in this second section, where the language seems to grow in bone density – is crunched into parataxis – and moves to a quicker beat, led by bolder imagery:

> and eternal Night
> Unchang'd; hoar Chaos and his ancient reign
> Dark, dismal; and vast Ocean's rushing might,
> From who the fluid air, each liquid plain,
> Each fountain flow'd, each river, and the boundless main.

('Song of the Creation')

Had Newton read *Paradise Lost*? 'Dark, dismal' would suggest so, as do the later lines: 'far beyond thy realm of light, / Beyond thy starry heav'ns'. Newton's introduction to a later book confirms this: 'The Author disclaims all eccentric views on the subject of prophecy. He has proof of this, only to mention the name … of Milton'. These echoes of Milton strengthen Newton's work, though he cannot improve on any aspect of *Paradise Lost* itself.

I've walked each of the dozen paths around the chapel, watching the building move like Google Street View; I realise now that I have passed Newton's headstone several times already. The text is fading, but the memorial itself is huge – a stone doorway facing the chapel. Matter energised by sun. There is an odd edge to the stone, like a pie crust. The lead letters are falling away.

The titles of Newton's later books demonstrate his interest in Biblical extremities, clashes between good and evil, and states of transformation. Newton is drawn to apocalypse and crash; *The Flight of the Apostate* (1849) is an early precursor to end of the millennium anxiety, which was still 150 years away when the book was published.

Newton's book isn't about our late 20th century millennial anxiety – Y2K, the Millennium Bug. His book instead rides the crest of Millenarianism, the belief system that the end of the millennium would bring epic transformation of some sort. Newton was convinced that this moment would bring a transformation, followed by redemption. It didn't matter that the people he preached to would never live to see it; they needed to act – and do it quickly. The millennium might bring utopia, but it would do so through destruction. Eden lies on the other side of Hiroshima. Much of this new belief system was based on The Book of Revelations: 'And I saw the dead, small and great, standing before God, and books were opened. And another book was opened, which is the Book of Life. And the dead were judged according to their works, by the things which were written in the books.'

There is no way to judge dead Victorian poets other than by their work; as always, I am here to find a revelation. I scan across the headstones in front of me, some of the 200,000 bodies buried in Abney Park – none of them raised as the millennium turned. A few – like Newton – left books behind.

Newton believed that the millennial transformation would not take the form of an appearance from Christ but would nevertheless be 'spiritual and providential'. He details the steps by which this millennial transformation will take place. Satan will be present, with his counterwork of 'fearfulness, trembling and horror', inducing despair in the individual; as God spreads light, Satan will attempt to 'darken, prevent and madden the public mind'. In this way, the space is cleared for 'social renovation ... a making "all things new"'. Newton is very specific about the timeframe for this, stating that 'his coming in person to raise the dead and judge the world, is a post-millenial event'.

The spring draws energy from the tail-end of a second lockdown. Another sparrow frisks over Newton's headstone. Sometimes I think of the Magnificent Seven as a network, and in this analogy, the tip of the chapel here could be a radio mast. When the chapel was first built, it was possible to see Highgate Cemetery from the roof. Node points connect the dark ring around a swelling city. Architecture has always figured in my dreams and my most recent is the strangest yet: I dreamt that Melania Trump was paying a visit to the Royal Gardens of Laeken (which she has done in real life – I have no idea how I know this) and she watches as the monumental greenhouse flies up into the sky.

As with many Millenarian visions, Newton's book is divided into three parts: 'Part I: The Judgement Hall of Antichrist'; 'Part II: The Flight of the Apostate' and 'Part III: The Cave of the Anarch, or, The Babel of England'. Newton's allegory is built on the construct that the Papacy is Antichrist ('Popery is an intruder from Ireland... spreading the shame of Antichrist'), his political supporters are 'the Beast', and that Rome is Babylon.

Newton believed that society was heading towards the 'eve of a great religious revival', which a religious poet will give voice to: 'a healthy reaction in his nature' to the 'poison'. The inference is that Newton *is* that poet.

It is one thing to engage with an epic work – which contains long, tedious sections – but quite another to read, in the introduction to the work itself, that the author already knows this. Newton writes of the 'The Cave of the Anarch' section:

> originally designed to be rather of a didactic character, with but little stirring description or action: he craves the reader's patience, till he has reached the 100th line of the second part, when interesting tidings from Rome reach the Archfiends, deliberating in their Judgment Hall on a matter of far inferior moment.

Why not cut the inferior moment all together, nix the didacticism, and start with the Archfiends?

Newton's poem attacks the 'mediocrity' of 'Time-serving journalists, whose papers enjoy the widest circulation, serving the times, serve Antichrist'. Newton sees the spread of substandard, hack-writing, as damaging to the nation's poetic legacy: 'If certain persons had the power, all over the land, of mixing arsenic with flour, in such quantities as to destroy gradually the digestive organs and the constitution, men would at last loathe the very name of bread, and shudder at the sight of a loaf'. For developing poets, self-awareness is crucial, and Newton is blind to the fact that he's baking penny loaves himself – not sourdough bloomers.

One of the flaws in the writing is that Newton deprives the reader of holding the work in their mind as a story, as well as an allegory, by constantly drawing their attention to his own conceit: 'The knowing looks of a conceited elf! / He is the critic'.

Despite this, I can't help enjoying Newton's conviction for his own main character – himself? – being dragged away to a cave of 'granite, dark, profound'. In the cave, Satan maintains that Albion is a lost cause, because he can find 'no fire of genius' amidst hack writers, and if his search proves fruitless, he will 'from that Albion's mind erase / All memory'. As with Milton – who Blake said 'was of the Devil's party without knowing it' – Newton teases out a compelling complexity in his Satan, who is a dynamic campaigner for good poetry over bad journalism. Newton's own enjoyment of this concept becomes infectious for the reader and leads to some of his finest lines of poetry: 'ether, with mephitic vapour charg'd / Darkled around me'.

The day is darkling around me. There is no lightning in Newton's work, but the ideas in the poems, along with the best lines – and his commitment to the ideas of spiritual apocalypse and transformation – is at the very least a mild storm. Right now, here in the cemetery, clouds are moving overhead, mephitic vapours, and I look down at the poems in front of me to find a startling couplet, buried in Newton's lost garden of words:

Ere millennial orient sun illumes
These verdant scenes

There is little sun to illumine the lead type on Newton's headstone, which is falling away to form another of the Magnificent Seven's concrete poems:

ovin Memory

The Rev   HIBB   NE   N
    WHO DIED
HE WAS A FAITHFUL PR HE   THE GOSPE
        AND   ALS AN   P
          HIS CH
THE TRIUMPH OF ISRAEL   WO
THE RIGHTFUL SHALL HINE FORTH AS THE SUN AN   KING

        ALSO OF
        ESTHER
     WIFE OF THE ABO

WHO ENTERED INTO REST ON NOVEMBER   19
"HIS MERCY IS ON THEM THAT DEAR HI

The evening chorus is in full song behind me, despite the clouds, and a lone gull is making a holding pattern above. But holding what? Somehow the whole cemetery appears in my mind, its millions of living things, each with its unique inscape. I look at the clock: five minutes to six. I hoof for the gates, before the garden closes me in.

The Garden of Laeken, 2020

Melania Trump pays a visit to the Royal Gardens of Laeken. It is the day of her 18th wedding anniversary to Donald. People should not be made to change, she thinks, they should be left as they are.

As she walks through the grounds – passing a rustling coterie of muslin, gold and perfume – a shadow appears above her. Melania looks up: the Iron Church, the most epic of the greenhouses, has detached from the gardens and is spinning beneath the sun, like a smelting disc. 'O my gawwwwd', she thinks, 'Donald will never believe this!'

Melania asks her assistant for her phone and she points it at the hovering structure: a Bismark helmet without a head. She takes 73 photos and a one-minute video, touching her left cheek with her other hand: it feels cool and lush after the morning's application of oxygen cream with vitamins A, C and E. Why do people never believe she was against botox – don't they know she would never do that to herself?

She looks around her team, hoping for an answer to the levitating greenhouse, which continues to spin above them. They are all pointing their cameras – Druids bleached by sun – their devices gleaming like tiny solar panels.

There was no clue as to what the hell was happening, on any of their faces, apart from perhaps the Trump Estate Communications Adviser, who had read only that morning that the Gardens of Laeken were commissioned by King Leopold II, who – through his own efforts – was the complete and outright owner of the Congo Free State.

Running Away from the Buried Year

So, here was the notion. What about a tale of a man who 'lost his way';
who became so entangled in some maze of imagination and speculation
that the common, material ways of the world became of no significance
to him? A fine notion, I think.

ARTHUR MACHEN, *THE LONDON ADVENTURE*

I CAN'T STOP RUNNING. The distances increase as the year rolls
on. Firstly, the nine miles through Liverpool's arid docks, Regent
Road, taking in the smell of waste, molasses and chemicals. Then
it's up to 12: out to Crosby Beach, standing in the nexus of the
Celtic world, looking out across Liverpool Bay, towards the Isle
of Man, surrounded by the Waves of Manannán. Beyond that:
Ireland. In the other direction are the hills of Wales – Talacre – a
seat of the ancient Bards. I had a lockdown dream that I flew there
– quite literally as the crow.

I have been re-reading *The Mabinogion*. The myth recounts
how Lludd, pre-Roman ruler of Britain, founds London ('Caer
Lludd'), but then three plagues destroy the peace. It is the first of

these plagues that interests me: the Coranaid, a race of beings, who come to Britain and cannot be forced out because their hearing is so good – they can hear anything the wind touches, making action against them futile. It is Llefelys who offers a solution for this, using a brass horn to prevent the Coranaid from hearing his conversation, revealing that they can be killed with a mixture made from a certain insect. The mixture is harmless to Britons, who must be covered in it at the same time as the Coranaid. I realise why the story compels me: aside from the near homophone of Coranaid/coronavirus, this is a fetishized vision of a vaccine. I am waiting to be covered with a virus killer – which in turn will give me access back to London.

A new national pastime begins: sea-talking. Loners, couples, families, emerge from creaking homes and stumble, like zombies, to the coast. One by one they walk forward to the great mother of the sea and talk to her. Pleas for mercy, broken hopes, indecipherable phrases – lockdown loops projected, at last, from the body. A litany extending along the country's coastline. I watch a couple in their 70s who have rehearsed this many times now: she walks into the sea, letting the cold waves wash over her toes. He is already bowed over a rockpool, checking his reflection is still there. Then they reconnect, staring out past the Wirral, the still centre between Celtic lands. There are a number of ships out there today and she raises binoculars, describing what she can see, as if the vaccine is in cargo. 'It's a big red one', she says – 'right there on the horizon'.

Do I come here to wave to the ghosts of poets? Joyce and Beckett over in Ireland, Hopkins and Dafydd ap Gwilym in Wales. Then the Wirral, an ancient plateau fronted by high-rise flats. Hello Malcolm Lowry. Ideas for fictionalised gardens come to me as I walk; I am reminded of Arthur Machen's declaration that we are made in order to seek adventure, an instinct that is as vital as drinking.

It could be the rejectamenta of the beach that draws me. During the never-ending January of 2021 I found a ticket for the Stena Line ferry from Liverpool to Belfast dated 23rd December 2020: an escapee – fleeing – in the tiny window of lifted restrictions. How did we end up like this, living like convicts? I looked closely at the ticket; it belonged to a woman: what was her story? Is she on the other side of this dystopia now? My passport has never been used so much – I need it to prove my age to the courier who delivers craft ales to my door. Those evenings with my wife Sarah have saved everything.

Then we both caught the virus: night-sweats, aching joints, chills. The house becomes a quarantine zone, food passed under the door to Pavel, aged 13, living ten days without human contact. The 'thing out there' was in my body, internal workings at war, body temperature testing out the function of my organs. An odd sense of being touched by momentous history, if only as a statistic – of quite literally *living through* the disease. The reality is less glamorous: binge-reading Patrick Hamilton novels, the London of the 1930s being all – in time and space – I can't get to, any time soon. Another courier, wanting us to take in a neighbour's parcel, who will not relent from my front door until I put my head through the window and say: 'we're a Covid household'. Retreat in a cloud of dust. The virus makes me lose my sense of smell – I try to imbibe the air now: sea without salt.

Anthony Gormley's *Another Place* surrounds me, a hundred iron men looking across the waves, waiting for an answer. The iron weeps to bronze, corrodes in auburns and greens. Rusticles, barnacles; a colonisation of marine life. Platelets of metal slide from the outer layers, burning under the scalding of light exposure. The statues wait; showroom dummies: wardens in watch for a dreadnought of hope.

This is a visionary place. It might have to do with its complete occupation by water, with people regularly being trapped by the incoming tide. Then there is the sinking mud, blackspots, pulling walkers down into the silt. The year is getting stranger: the collective consciousness of the nation has transformed a 100-year-old former British Army officer into a temporary God. Captain Tom is walking laps of his own garden. The pandemic has opened a rip in time, where the ancient laws of magic can govern again. James George Frazer, in *The Golden Bough*, describes how locals in Cambodia (at the time of his writing) would respond to an epidemic by going out with a band of music to look for a man whom the local God has chosen as a temporary incarnation. 'When found, the man is conducted to the altar of the god, where the mystery of incarnation takes place. Then the man becomes an object of veneration to his fellows, who implore him to protect the village against plague'. So we have Captain Tom.

During lockdown, more and more people have been getting rescued from the mud here, pushing their daily exercise further, driven by the id towards a death of their own choosing – breaking the seal on repetition – feeling the mud take their legs. The worst thing you can do is struggle. Ankles and hips break. And worse; there's always the chance that the lifeguards will think you're one of Gormley's replicants.

Crosby beach is familiar and alien; millions of years of weather trapped in the one place, a war between erosion and life. A few months after the virus broke out, I met the poet James Byrne here on the beach. When I arrived, he was sat in the sand, in grief for his brother Robin who had died in the April of the first lockdown. James was sitting side-on to the sea, his bike tossed to the elements: reading Sebald's *Austerlitz*. We were the first friend either of us had seen in months.

Herman Melville once met Nathaniel Hawthorne just a few miles along the beach from here, in Southport. Melville was on another of his journeys, itching for an answer, glossy-eyed and unboundaried. *Moby Dick* had been published five years before and had been panned by the critics. Hawthorne later wrote that Melville had 'pretty much made up his mind to be annihilated'. Open mudflats; the desolation of sandhills. The wind can be brutal here.

Then I read about Sou Zen Young, who drowned here in 1910. He was forty years old, his death an act of political radicalism. Working under various aliases, he had tried to overthrow the Qing Dynasty in China, aiming to replace it instead with the 'three principles' of Democracy, Nationalism and Social Justice. Escaping earlier imprisonment in 1904, he had planned to assassinate the Empress Dowager Cixi between Beijing's Forbidden City and the Summer Palace, but security was too controlled. He continued to work covertly, blinding himself in one eye while manufacturing explosives. Then he came to the UK to raise funds for his revolutionary forces. It was here he met Sun-Yat-sen, who would later become the first president of the

Republic of China; they discussed strategies for a future China. But why did Sou Zen Young drown himself here, walking out into the silvery light and blackspots?

It is hard to know how personal collapse leads to suicide; Sou Zen Young was apparently broken by reports of heavy revolutionary losses in China, and might have been compelled by the idea of a martyr's suicide, one that would add ballast to the political cause. He was also living through the loss of an eye, mental illness, life fatigue. His dead body was pulled out from the sea by local fishermen; a formless statue, observed by the ancient light and hawking gulls.

By chance I discover that he is buried in my local cemetery, Anfield. A Victorian creation, opened in 1863, this space was invented with the same impulse as London's Magnificent Seven: to take pressure off the city's overcrowded, central burial grounds. The map of its design reminds me of the body of a Hymenoptera: catacombs buried in the exoskeleton. The outer paths are forewings.

It is said that when drug addicts move home, they draw dealers to their doorstep. Cut off from London, and Abney Park, I soon gravitated towards Anfield Cemetery, taking my daily headlines from the headstones. It starts with a jog through the heat of my

43rd birthday, pounding through the vapours of work frustration – redundancies, uncertainty, union politics – the pandemonium of the crisis. Then Pavel and I meet my mum here; I listen as they talk of how they're missing each other – a year wasted – with none of their usual adventures, holidays, sleepovers. It takes nearly a year, and a quote from a Spanish columnist, to make me realise just how much harder things are for Pavel. Like a juvenile goshawk, baby feathers yet to fall – wide-eyed and lean – Pavel's voice is breaking; a high-pitched call here, a bass note there. I start to worry about the long-term effects on him, this year that he'll never get back: experience in stasis.

Family is amoeba: one cell moves, the other adapts. It is a living grief, this garden of longing; the need to live fully, to experience *now*, against the law of social distancing. Time dripping its black tallow, embalming the trapped body.

My mum walks slowly alongside me, impossible that she's seventy. The cancer of five years ago scared us, then she caught Covid – her body holding on through the night sweats. She's been waiting for the spring to break, to move out of social distancing. The three of us walk through the cemetery, past the obelisk for EDWARD JOHN, 'who was accidentally drowned in the Ribble' in 1892. Pavel and my mum talk of all the good times, and tentative plans to come – because who knows what might still happen, now we're stacking the bricks of our hopes on fluid foundations? Japanese spindle trees surround us; blue surgical masks appear at the edges of the paths. Early crocuses. Three squirrels unreel in front of us – cup their hands in prayer – respool towards a tree.

We walk past the Chinese graves, the new headstones multiplying. I see something on the floor and pick it up: a handwritten letter, unravelling in pages of externalised subconscious. A eulogy of trapped love, written for someone living, or perhaps dead:

> So much always trying for you   everyday in life   good
>   things   like you should try   in the park all day   it's
> 14th March   of this month   hurry up hurry up

An abstruse invocation to the spring, a letter to the elements, aiming to lift the months of cold and dark – to light up the garden that's been buried inside. I put the letter back in its envelope – which is also entirely covered with words and hearts – and leave it in a rhododendron bush.

That evening I feel exhausted, the spring pushing through my limbs; the first buds, forcing their way through hard earth. Altering the image of everything – spring is almost here.

Rested, I run to Crosby Beach again – walking on the

mudflats. I walk past two men tangled in lockdown hair, and one of them uses the word 'annihilation'.

Then the government announce that the lockdown restrictions are lifting again, and I feel the pull of Abney Park.

The Garden of the Egyptian Dead, 1102 BC

May my body be given back to me   my arms   my legs
My eyes which have seen so many things   even my enemies
My head shaped like a jackal thinned at the back by wildfire
My body that is clad in panther skin with a ram-headed snake
My mouth which has unleavened so many breads   the rings of my words
My long covid wearing purple trousers

I am Abney-Anubis   mouth and scribe of all the Gods
Triumphant overseer of the Underworld
Come from the Pool of Fire   to quench that fire

Extinction is Not Death

—— JOSIAH CONDER

No; we see nothing at all; though poets catch strange glimpses of reality,
now and then, out of the corners of their eyes.
ARTHUR MACHEN, *THE LONDON ADVENTURE*

I'M BACK AT THE GATES, on a two-fold quest: to walk the landscape which once held a magnificent tree, the Cedar of Lebanon, and to find the grave of poet Josiah Conder (1789-1855). Conder is buried somewhere within the roots of this ghost tree. The *Morning Advertiser* of 5th January 1856 reported: 'The mortal remains of Josiah Conder were yesterday committed to the earth, in a new grave at the higher end of Abney Park Cemetery, near the spot marked by the cedar tree which adorns that place of sepulchre'. I check my map as I walk, easily identifying the island of which the tree was king; the architecture of the path is still a fixture in the cemetery. It is dense with foliage, poplars, holly, vines, rhododendrons – fighters for the light.

Conder was born into a family of dissenters; his father ran a bookshop in London. Conder's childhood was marred by smallpox, which caused him to lose sight in his right eye. After receiving electrical treatment which was believed to stop the disease from spreading, he recovered and was then sent to be educated at the dissenting academy in Hackney. Subsequently, he took over the running of the family bookshop. The work gave him time to write and, at the age of 17, lines from his poem 'The Withered Oak' appeared in the *Athenæum*, edited by Theodore Watts-Dunton, whose Putney home I wrote about in *In the Catacombs*. The more I walk the Magnificent Seven, the more intricate the poetic web becomes.

The Cedar of Lebanon also received its own coverage, with the *Uxbridge & W. Drayton Gazette* reporting on 14th October 1865: 'It is a splendid specimen, and is now laden with thousands of cones in various stages of growth, the contrast between the colour of which, especially the younger ones, and the very dark foliage of the trees, is very charming, and as far as I know, very unusual in the immediate vicinity of London'.

There is a particular poem by Josiah Conder which hints at strangeness, as if saying something about the transitory portal of Abney Park:

In that sudden, strange transition,
    By what new and finer sense

Shall we grasp the mighty vision,
　And receive its influence?
Angels, guard the new immortal
　Through the wonder-teeming space,
To the everlasting portal,
　To the spirit's resting-place.

(from 'The Reverie', Part II)

Conder is another of Abney's polymaths – an editor of *The Eclectic Review* – writing poetry, hymns, travel and religious prose. His 30-volume non-fiction work *The Modern Traveller* (1824) is an example of journeying without movement, a book detailing every continent, written by someone who never left Great Britain.

There is a painting of Conder by Benjamin Robert Haydon showing the poet at the 1840 Anti-Slavery Society Convention, an event that Conder co-organised; he is painted amongst the crowd, collars up and eyes alert. Conder interrogated slavery from different angles: through organising conventions, by writing a prose book outlining the economic flaws of slavery, and through his poems:

Oh, what of the night?
Doth the Crucifix bend?
When shall glimmer the light

This gross darkness end?
Deep in the Pacific has sunk the last gleam
That o'er the dark horrors of bondage might stream.

('The Last Night of Slavery')

The image of the crucifix bending here is startling. Conder glosses
the line to explain that the Southern Constellation appeared to
bend at midnight, but the image also works as a statement for
how wrong slavery should appear to people of religious faith. The
poem has ensured Conder's legacy in print, being republished in
the 1999 anthology, *Slavery, Abolition and Emancipation: writings
in the British Romantic Period*. It is around this cause that Conder
would write some of his best work.

Outside the cemetery walls, cars are purring. The wind picks up
– as if to combat the machines. A pile of logs, like a hearth, has
been piled in front of me. Perhaps cremation is the ritual for me?
It was the way my paternal grandfather chose to go. Two hours
in a cremation chamber, the body burned at 2,000 °F. There are
options for the remains to be attached to a firework or blasted
from a canon like Hunter S. Thompson (which apparently cost
his friend Johnny Depp $3 million). I can understand why my

dad broke the family line and was buried. Cremation is not good for the environment (every cremation uses around 16 gallons of fuel, pumping dioxins into the air). Obliteration, reduction to dust. My father went for a coffin; the feel of its weight on my shoulder: grief's counterweight.

In his lifetime, Conder was best known for his anthology of hymns, *The Congregational Hymn Book* (1844), which sold 90,000 copies in its first seven years of publication. This book contained his own hymns, as well as those by well-known hymnologists such as Isaac Watts, whom Conder described as 'The Poet of the Sanctuary'. I decide to take the long route to Conder's memorial, leaving the path behind me, and step into the island of undergrowth once occupied by the Cedar of Lebanon. George Collison gave a loving description of this tree:

> This beautiful and appropriate tree will at once be admitted to be one of the finest specimens we have of the species; and it excels many of its contemporaries in height, the circumference of its stem, and of its longitudinal branches. The health and vigour of this monarch of trees are surprising when its age is considered ... Its age is nearly 200 years, and I believe that few older English specimens exist.

Collison recounts the story of the mower's scythe that was placed against its trunk and forgotten; when the surrounding vegetation was pulled way, the handle of the scythe was still visible. The tree lived for nearly a hundred years after Collison's account.

It takes just five steps to make London disappear; I am lost on the dead cedar's island. Stillness. Trilling of birdsong. A woodlouse, slowly rowing – an endless eviction. I come across a blue plaque for Peter Salter, former friend and Chairman of Abney Park; it hovers like a flag from a moon landing.

Dappled sunbeams waver across the earth. Trefoils loll. A bee, furious and heavy, blunders through the silence. The leaves of Spanish bluebells are peeled back, as if ringing with sound. I cross over a path that runs through the island – a hidden equinox buried in this English rock garden.

It was as a poet that Conder first wanted to be known, writing in the preface to his collection *The Star in the East* (1824): 'the contents of this little volume are the casual production of leisure hours, during the last twelve years. Some of them have, at intervals, found their way into print ... poetry has long ceased to be with me more than a record of feeling, and a source of quiet enjoyment.'

Twelve years later, his 'literary pursuits' had come to fully preoccupy him, writing in the preface to his next collection, *The Choir and the Oratory* (1837), that poetry had 'occupied me so incessantly as to leave few intervals' for anything else. Conder's verse improved with age, his ability to condense ideas into images grew in tandem with his authority over language. As the title suggests, his poetic interests were moving towards psalmody and hymnody, but his practice also consists of the opposite: moving the original Psalms into metrical verse – repurposed in the spirit of 'the best translators' – to be read on the page. It is interesting that Conder stumbles here on the modern practice of 'expanded translation'. Conder's versions of the psalms are not presented to be sung – like Isaac Watts' – but to present 'the specific character of the particular psalm'.

This growing commitment to poetry took place amidst personal tragedy. One poem was written after the death of an infant son. The boy appears before Christ: 'There stands our child before the Lord, / In royal vesture drest'. Conder took his joy in another child, 'E.R.C (the merriest of babes)': 'The time will come – it must be so – / The world shall cloud thy childish bliss'. Conder makes no great claims for these poems of occasions – one written for a sister's birthday, another about his recovery from illness. They are simple lyrics, written for family first, audience later. They recount the despair and joys of life in his 20s and 30s.

A man splutters somewhere behind me: covert smoker or another Covid revenant? I have waited so long to be back in the cemetery and now I am here, I have marooned myself.

Stylistically, Conder's poetry is held back by its archaic constructions, the influence of 17th-century phrasing – 'Bear thou', 'Witness ye', 'laughter obscene' – which detract from poems of otherwise compelling world-making:

> In the furthest deserts of the deep,
> The coral-worm its architecture vast
> Uprears, and new-made islands have their birth

The image of the coral worm is presented on an epic scale, the detail is vivid and arresting, but the impact is diminished by the phrasing of 'architecture vast' – why not 'vast architecture'? Wordsworth and Coleridge's *Lyrical Ballads* had been published 39 years before, demonstrating how everyday speech could become soluble matter for the creation of poetry.

Conder was fierce in his independence, writing in *On Protestant Nonconformity* (1818): 'The Author has not written with the view of pleasing a party, nor yet with the ambitious hope of operating a change in the opinions of those who entertain opposite views of the subject.' It is this singularity of vision which strengthened his ideas on the pending religious transformation to come, which he expanded upon in his series of poems, 'The

Apocalypse'. This was so popular that he wrote an accompanying commentary called *The Harmony of History with Prophecy: an exposition of the Apocalypse* (1849). The Victorian public loved to believe that they were on the verge of spiritual transformation, and the clearer – and more dramatic – these artistic depictions of the Second Coming were, the better. Conder's *The Harmony of History* is a 500-page exposition of 'Revelations', interrogating every word and symbol of the text, holding each potential portent up to the light.

Conder had a clear view of what the Apocalypse would entail: Witnesses, Trumpets, Vials and – against the view of many others – the belief that the 'Ten-horned Beast' would appear. Conder's writing on the Apocalypse is the most erudite and well researched of all Abney's dissenters, but it is research fused with his own visionary intuition. He believed that six of the seven vials of the angels had been poured, and that he was living on the verge of the seventh – and the final trumpet. A lockdown revenant, I think of the significance of those vials being filled with plague – cups pouring out the wraths of God. Revelations are commonly believed to be transmitted by dream or spiritual epiphany, but they can also travel via another channel: poetry. The revelatory poem is a conduit for prophecies.

The sun pushes through the layers of green above and

warms my neck. Through a gap in the trees, I can see the source itself. In the time since I entered the island, new light has reached me. I have only moved five metres. Light is revelation. A few days ago, I dreamt that I was seeing the first ever storm. It fell in huge drops, puncturing the sand of an arid, primordial landscape, as lizards watched the genesis of the world's first garden.

What does Conder's poetic Apocalypse entail? Jesus has a central place, arriving in person 'amid the clouds'. Six trumpets have sounded and a throne is lit in heaven, around which are 'mystic shapes' denoting 'the general host of God's redeemed'. Conder follows the book of Revelations chronologically but embellishes this, describing Famine on a black horse: 'marked by the scales that weigh the precious seed'. 'Storm ... fire, and plague' descend. As in the Bible, a fifth angel sends a star from heaven, which 'unlock[s] the abyss bituminous'. 'Their prey is men'. Conder compacts whole sections of the narrative of 'Revelations' to just a few lines of poetry, condensing key symbols – actions and events – into images that keep the pace moving. The dragon of the Bible is interpreted by Conder as 'Papal Babylon / Receiv[ing] her doom'. Conder, like his cemetery-mate, Hibbert Newton, suggests that the Second Coming will destroy Papacy. His vision is one of London transformed by upheaval, with each street of the city holding the potential to become a portal, a worm tunnel for the resurrection of the dead:

> The elements shall melt with fervent heat.
>> Earth's central fires shall pierce the fragile crust [...]
> A fairer globe shall from the skies invite
>> The bridal city on that day of days.
> Lo, built on truth, and walled with glorious might,
>> Its pearly gates each golden street displays.
> God is its temple, and the Lamb its light;
>> Love the pure element, the language praise.

> (X, 'The Apocalypse')

I move further into the island, dipping low under a poplar branch, feeling the ground with each step before finding purchase. The feeling is akin to floating, the abandonment of closed spaces; the way nature absorbs the body, knowing it is part of what it is itself. Green alkanet is at my feet, a sub-species of the forget-me-not family: five petalled shots of blue-purple. Something moves heavily through the undergrowth, then freezes. I imagine its heart, beatboxing against canvas.

Conder loved nature too and his 'Sacred Poems' are direct, eulogistic poems of praise, interpreting natural elements such as the sea or a comet as evidence of God's divinity and goodness.

Standing in Abney's verdant arboretum, I think of Conder as a reveller in the natural world, a man who took time to pause – to watch – and to capture what he saw in language:

> The landscape is alive: the shadows fly …
> A dotting scarce perceptible, thrown out
>   In tints of livelier brown, on hedge and bough,
> Gives mystic signs.
>
> (from 'Spring: in four sonnets')

Conder's poetry grasps at the unknown, capturing the voice of an oak tree, or a harp heard in the night. 'It seems to speak of all to me / In vocal poetry'.

Then the illusion breaks: the island I'm lost in turns out to be no more than twenty metres across. It has taken me half an hour to wade through its entanglements, to find the path in front of me. A bald man in John Lennon sunglasses walks in front of me, staring directly back into my face, like a shadow that has followed me from Liverpool.

We know what was said at Conder's funeral, as the officiating cleric, the Reverend John Harris, published his sermon under the title *The Divine Rest* (1856): 'A TOMB has been described as a monument placed on the boundary of two worlds. Standing, at this moment, as at the grave of departed worth, we command a view of both worlds – of heaven and earth, time and eternity. In which direction shall we first look?'

Conder chose to look both ways at once, writing in his poem 'Death':

> Extinction is not death. Its fading leaves
>   The tree deplores not, nor resents its fall.
> The insect feels no pang…
> Death is cessation, and not punishment.
>
> Creative Opulence can well sustain
>   This waste and flow of reproductive life,
> In wondrous scale; and nothing lives in vain.

This is the writing of a man who has made his peace with death, seeing it as one stage in a continuum. He clearly believed that 'Creative Opulence' could counterbalance the eventual waste of the body. The suggestion here is that his poetry will be made to count, and someone – like me – will find it in the future.

Back on the path, I am edging away from the ghost tree, towards the spot where Conder is buried. A sudden rush of cow parsley has turned the area around the grave into a snowfield. I lean into it, holding the memorial of James Esdaile, died 1864 – HE BEING DEAD YET SPEAKETH – searching for the poet. Wrong turn. The sanctuary is long behind me now and I have entered broken, arid terrain – memorials sinking into earth – potholes and broken stones.

I retreat and re-enter a few metres down the path, this time galvanised by the sight of hazard tape. My foot slides down into the grave of a David Edward Lambert, and I pull it out, grabbing onto ivy and a hunk of dry earth. I am instantly here: the low-lying hip tomb of Josiah Conder is in front of me, a slab of pale grey. The memorial gave little thought for future readers, with the text being too low to the ground to read. This is the way it goes with dead poets: wait centuries for a reader, then there's been a formatting error. I press the torch on my phone, but the letters are no clearer than hieroglyphs, a crochet of 'C's and 'X's. I try the other side but can only distinguish a single word: ELIZABETH.

I leave Josiah Conder there, with his wife. Their grave is lit by white bluebells.

The Garden of Perpetual Rain, 300 million BC

It started after drought   A thousand years of earthburn   Insects
lived off a speck of humidity in a lizard's eye   What the lizards lived
off is unknown   their arms rigid as Pompeii's priests   they would
raindance   if there was music

Then there *was* music   first the tin peel of a drop   its pea-sized
pendulum shook the canyons   then another   plotting its spot in
the sand   then a third   giving form to the others   it rang out
the grizzled pip that hits the spittoon   clones followed   battalions
of angels   carrying vials   bowls without virus   spilling themselves
without mercy   whale songs of love   wanting to explode
imploding   in dust   each in solace to the psycho sun   that knew
what it had done   but had swallowed its own neck   knowing what
had been done to *it*   you do not ask for that   each drop was
solace   shining   the lizards licked their backs   they had no word
for this   it was raining

The Luminous Web & Saints of Hackney

—— EMILY BOWES GOSSE

It is a debatable point, I suppose, whether life, taking it all round, by and large … is a horrible business. On the one hand, most of us are excessively sorry to quit this world, so, clearly, there must be something to be said for it.

ARTHUR MACHEN, *THINGS NEAR AND FAR*

THERE WAS A STRAIN of Victorianism that was so repressed the human skeleton glowed in the dark. Oscillation between resurrectionist euphoria and Sundays spent scouring the family Bible. Movement through an open window. A moth lands on Genesis. This was the kind of tension that John Fowles satirised in *The French Lieutenant's Woman*; a lone woman walking the seafront before a male viewer: desire snagged in green tweed. These tensions orchestrated the life of Emily Bowes Gosse (1806-1857) and her husband Philip. Due to their son's best-selling 'study' of their life and beliefs, published as *Father and Son* (1907), we have the clearest document of any poet I have discovered in the Magnificent Seven. I'm here today to consider Gosse's poetry and to find her headstone.

This northern part of the cemetery is bramble territory; Little Elm Walk is a misnomer. A robin stops on the stone in front of me, looking up, down: tin soldier. It was her son Edmund who wrote Gosse's entry for the *Dictionary of National Biography*; an objective squib of forced praise:

> She was a woman of somewhat unusual acquirements, a fair Greek and a good Hebrew scholar, and one of the earliest of the modern 'workers in the East End.' She died in London on 9 Feb. 1857, after a very painful illness.

Gosse was born in the capital in 1806 and later lived with her parents in Clapton, where she attended the Plymouth Brethren assembly. It was here that she met the preacher and naturalist Philip, whom she married in 1848. What Edmund's stark biography leaves out is the fact that Emily Gosse wrote numerous books herself; she was a polymath, a landscape painter as well as a poet and a religious writer in prose.

The chemical reek of Victorian baking soda and vinegar couldn't be further from Abney today. Corvus wars in the trees above, a rattle of competing syrinx. Where is Gosse's grave? I was told to look for a tall, arched design, its plain grey texture now mottled to green. A glow-in-the-dark shield. In 1966 Robert Boyd, Gosse's biographer, was here: 'The grave looked neglected, but still standing nearby was the ancient elm tree … its trunk having grown to more than three feet in diameter when I saw it'. Like the Cedar of Lebanon, this huge elm is no longer here.

Emily Gosse wrote dozens of gospel tracts, published by the Weekly Tract Society. Her posthumously published *Narrative Tracts* (1864) is estimated to have been distributed to seven million people. 'The Two Maniacs: A True Story' was written for working class readers in an attempt to bring any straying souls back to the fold of Jesus. Gosse had completed missionary work in the East End and was intimate with the levels of drunkenness and guttural language spoken amongst the poor. Gosse's text describes a group of men who visit a cemetery to 'pass around the jovial cup'. To show his fearlessness, one man attempts to call up the dead, and in that moment a 'white object' appears from behind a tomb, saying 'Yes, Lord, I come! I come!' The man flees and loses his mind: 'he had lost his reason, which he never again recovered . . . [he] passed the remainder of his days in the madhouse'. To ensure that readers didn't project a supernatural reading onto the narrative, Gosse tells us that the 'white object' was in fact an old woman, resting between the graves, who thought the voice was an Archangel's call and went to meet the summoner.

I look around the graves here: bramble and bindweed. Cemeteries excite visions, and my mind is ahead of me now, remembering Machen's tale of 'The White People'. 'Sorcery and sanctity', the tale begins, 'these are the only realities'.

Gosse loved nature. She wrote a collaborative book of prose with Philip, entitled *Sea-Side Pleasures* (1853). Gosse's love of the coast was rooted in her childhood when she had spent much of her time in Wales. Due to Phillip's work, they visited the sea together, where he could work on his studies and she could write or paint the landscape. The couple were clearly very close, though there is something strained in the working relationship. Philip had invented the word 'Aquarium' for his hugely popular book, *The Aquarium: an unveiling of the wonders of the deep sea* (1854), and Emily's vivid chromolithographs played a huge part in the book's success; but in the published book an acknowledgement for her contribution was absent. The title page reads 'By Henry Gosse, A.L.S. etc' and is followed by an epitaph: '"The sea is HIS life, and He made it" – Ps. Xcv. 5.'

I stumble on the edge of something solid and look down: the edge of a flat grave, that reads, through trailing ivy: ALSO HIS WIFE. One option for my own burial is to leave my body to medical science, which could help advance care for the living and those yet to come. But then I think of the students in white coats, dapping indigo squares onto my flesh, under the shadow of a shaky scalpel. I have my doubts; it is not a death on earth that appeals.

One of Gosse's sketches of the sharp, rocky landscape of Byng Cliff, Dorset, shows a man in a long coat and top hat edging further towards the sea, his coat the same wet black as the rocks. The spectre of Philip Gosse, her husband, chasing his obsession into the sea – towards the jaws of fame. After she died, Philip wrote a book called *Omphalos* (1857), which challenged the views of Lyle and Darwin by arguing that God created the tracks of evolution so that 'the world presented, instantly, the structural appearance of a planet on which life had long existed'. The book was shot down from both sides, naturalists and Christians. As Charles Kingsley wrote to Philip to explain, after 25 years of geological study he was not prepared to 'believe that God has written on the rocks one enormous and superfluous lie'. Edmund later wrote about his father: 'He could not recover from amazement at having offended everybody by an enterprise which had been undertaken in the cause of universal reconciliation'.

Emily Bowes Gosse has since been written about so much, scripted into cultural memory, her body documented from every angle. Anna Shipton – another tract writer and a friend of Emily – later published a book called *Tell Jesus: Recollections of Emily Gosse and Poems* (1863). Sycophantic in tone and message, the book is an account of Gosse's life and faith; I doubt even reviewers of the time, including the *Washington Post* believed all of it: 'In this delightful narrative of Christian experience we have an example of working for Jesus and being happy, of suffering bodily affliction and being happy, and of dying and being happy'. Edmund Gosse wrote in *Father and Son*: 'For nearly three months I breathed the atmosphere of pain, saw no other light, heard no other sounds'. Shipton writes about her first meeting with Gosse:

> I was still groping in the twilight of spiritual dawn when I first met Emily Gosse. She appeared to me then, as she lives in the memory of this hour, as one of God's epistles … She was fair, and appeared more youthful than her years, from her small delicate features, and the artless, childlike smile which lighted her countenance when animated.

For Shipton, she was delicate and angelic, for Edmund she became an abstract creature of pain, who became strange to him through illness. For Philip she was a subject – a human specimen. Dennis Potter's television play *Where Adam Stood* (1976) is about the Gosse family and lingers over a portrait of Emily which hangs on a wall in the family home. Over her left shoulder is a ship, painted on the horizon; a reference to Edmund Gosse's complaint that his parents never allowed him fairy tales or toys. 'Around my tender and unconscious spirit was flung the luminous web', Edmund Gosse wrote, referring to his Christian indoctrination: 'the light and elastic but impermeable veil'.

Emily Gosse's poetry collections never reached a wide audience, and her tracts are now only viewed as historical documents. But Shipton's book was reprinted at least sixty times until 1931, selling over 307,000 copies, proving that there is something that people found inspiring in Gosse's life. Edmund's book is still in print with Oxford World Classics. He is buried six miles away in East Finchley Cemetery. Phillip is on the other side of the country, in Torquay Cemetery. The family is divided by split loyalties, a force stronger than geography.

Two women walk past with bottles of Punk IPA, heading towards Watts' Mound, their conversation swirling towards the graves in fragments: 'Like whisky and ... everything they did was amazing ... it was like, *live* experience'.

Edmund went against his father's advice to become – like his mother – a poet. Today he is not a poet known for originality or for a continued readership, with his collections being out of print since the 1920s. Although published by some of the biggest publishers of his time – Kegan Paul & Co. and W. Heinemann – a topsoil has grown over his work. His contribution to poetry was in popularising the villanelle form. Like so many Victorian writers, his books are now coming back in print-on-demand editions; a defibrillated corpus, resurrected by BiblioLife Reproduction Series. In all my time at the National Poetry Library I have only responded to one enquiry relating to Edmund Gosse, when someone was looking for his poem 'The Wallpaper'. The poem takes its force from the body of his mother, describing one of her final acts of strength in lifting up her boy:

> When I was only five years old,
>   My mother, who was soon to die,
> Raised me with fingers soft and cold,
>   On high;
>
> Until, against the parlour wall,
>   I reached a golden paper flower.
> How proud was I, and ah! how tall,
>   That hour!

It would be a mistake to believe that cemeteries don't move; in reality they slide, contract, expand – forcing memorials to change position. Human testaments shaken by geology. The stone wants to say: I am fixed – like literary reputation – but beneath it the earth is unstable. Has Gosse's grave been lost to this shifting landscape?

Edmund Gosse's attack on his parents was the creation of unreconstructed hurt. After his father's death, Edmund learned that his own birth was documented in his father's journal as: 'E. delivered of a son. Received green swallow from Jamaica'. Emily Gosse later wrote in her journal: 'We have given him to the Lord … if the Lord take him early, we will not doubt that he is taken to Himself'. Extreme devotional sacrifice of this kind borders on the occult: the child offered to God, a votive of spirited obsession. Emily withdrew from the Plymouth Brethren, or what she describes as 'the saints of Hackney', writing: 'I have made up my mind to give myself up to Baby for the Winter'. Edmund Gosse would later describe being taken with his mother on her mysterious expeditions, to connect the lost souls of London with God: 'I recollect pleasant rambles through the City by her side, and the act of looking up at her figure soaring above me'.

It is through these details that we get the clearest picture of who Emily was – a woman living under a master narrative – but also a person driven by kindness and care for others: 'Her manners were so gentle and persuasive, she looked so innocent, her small sparkling features were so lighted up with so much benevolence, that I do not think she ever met with discourtesy or roughness'. Then cancer comes between the child and his mother: 'Now, and for the first time in my life, I no longer slept in her room, no longer sank to sleep under her kiss … I felt … I had shrunken into a very small and insignificant figure, that she was floating out of reach … and a great, blind anger against I knew not what awakened in my soul.' How much of Edmund's book is written as an unconscious attempt to give him leverage over that sick bed – to be seen and heard – and take control of his rage?

I step back onto the path, trying to find another angle, a different perspective from which to spot her grave, but I make the mistake of catching the eye of a passing Staffordshire Bull Terrier. It grits its teeth, spits, barks. I take the standing approach for a while. No sudden movements. 'Poppy!' the owner shouts, but she's on her phone and already miles down the path. Poppy is refusing to roll back her top lip until I move ground. I walk down the path, towards the chapel – help me God – but she follows, foaming white at the mouth. Eventually she gives up – victorious – striding with a swagger towards her owner. Bone earned.

In his invective, Edmund Gosse hits low with his pandy bat: 'Mother also was a writer, author already of two slender volumes of religious verse – the earlier of which, I know not how, must have enjoyed some slight success, since a second edition was printed …. Neither of them knew nor cared about any manifestation of current literature.' Edmund says that neither of his parents had read a poet since Byron. Reading is the key to writerly success, and just as there cannot be a successful scientist who is not grounded in the latest thinking in their field, the same applies to poets. Poets who don't read are not protected from their false Eurekas. Did the poetry of Emily Gosse suffer from this limitation in her own reading?

We have in Emily Gosse another of Abney's hymnologists. Due to the straightforward language and controlled expression of her poetry, the work on the page seems incomplete without musical accompaniment. Gosse was not interested in creating a singular style of voice, which would have contradicted her aim of expressing love for God:

> Almighty father! give us grace,
> The works of darkness hence to chase,
>   And every thought of ill;
> Arouse us from dreams of night,
> Array us with the arms of light,
>   And mould us to thy will.

('A Collect for First Sunday Advent')

Unlike Hopkins, who wanted to stand before God and give praise through – and *for* – his individuality, Gosse is writing poetry that is 'moulded' to God's will. By extension, the work must then take pre-moulded forms, and make no distraction from the almighty force that she is guided by. This forgets that the most compelling poems of faith come from a dialogue with God; Gosse's work is a simple record of what she has received from above. The work is at its best when Gosse allows some level of doubt to be aired, and although this is never a doubting of God, she does often question her own actions . There is pathos in her poem 'An Evening Hymn', which gives praise for her health at the time of writing:

> Has health been mine? I thank thee, Lord,
>   For this and every gift.
> To thee, for all thou dost afford,
>   My heart in praise I lift:
>   That heart retain!
>   For ne'er again
> Would I be led by trifles vane.

> (from 'An Evening Hymn')

There is an echo of George Herbert here:

> Since my sadnesse
> Into gladnesse
> Lord thou dost convert,
>   O accept
>   What thou has kept,
> As thy due desert.

(From 'An Offering')

Like Herbert, Gosse adopts indented lines that oscillate in length. If she had not read any poets since Byron, there is a suggestion that she had learned about poetic form from significant earlier writers such as Herbert.

I find myself back in a netherworld of graves: same garden, different angle. The sun dulls; clouds pause; the sky opens in a flash storm. Dry plates of ivy seem to fry in the sudden torrents. Abney's garden moves in the invisible flow – accepting whatever it can get – and the elms seem to race upwards, tense, anticipating a shot of moisture. Raindrops run down the side of a strong, grey, granite obelisk. Tendrils of ivy fold around its edges. Every surface here is a platform for life to touch, to find purchase, to proliferate. A fallen elm is at my feet, the casualty of a storm, its bark textured and leathery, pitted with the evidence of its past resilience. Its insides exposed – but not in clean, evidential rings; there are signs of an enforced end, with its phloem – that word which echoes 'poem' – long since ceasing to pass food to the tree. It has hardened to bark, its sapwood twisted at the point of destruction. Heartwood mangled.

Philip Gosse took a forensic approach to the body of his dying wife, writing *A Memorial of the Last Days on Earth of Emily Gosse* (1857). There is something powerful and moving in this account of her last breathing hours, the result of breast cancer, at a point in history when treatments were limited, bordering barbaric: 'About the end of April, 1856, my beloved Emily became conscious of a hard lump in her left breast, the first intimation of that dreadful disease, which was commissioned to dissolve her earthly house of this tabernacle in nine short months'. Nine months: death echoes gestation. Philip Gosse's book is a studied attempt to understand the disease that killed his wife at a time when the disease was stigmatised: 'We saw that when the doctor applied his fingers, there was a separation, all round, of the dead tumour from the healthy flesh'. Philip was known to spend 20 minutes static at a time, eye glued to a microscope. Emily had chosen not to have a mastectomy but to be treated via caustics; her husband describes her being passed from doctor to doctor in an attempt to find a diagnosis. The wife with whom he had collaborated on studies of nature now becomes his scientific subject: 'the great insensible tumour fell out of its cavity, hanging only by a slender fleshy thread, which presently yielded, and the breast was relieved of its load – the dead body that it had so long carried about'. The cancer spreads into a 'mass about as large as a hen's egg', he writes, as hope of a cure disappears.

Yesterday I fell asleep in the afternoon and dreamt of a garden of invisible trees; it was a macabre, unsettling dream – not a bit like standing here now, enlivened by a sudden shower. Somewhere far off, a car blisters the air with its horn; the sound of a children's playground. There are 20 minutes until the cemetery gates close. Where is Emily? Sometimes there is no epiphany, no white object that emerges from between headstones to lead the way. Emily's final words were: 'I shall walk with Him in white. Won't you take our lamb and walk with me?'

Although Gosse published two volumes of verse in her lifetime, neither of them are in the British Library. Her poems are only available due to Robert Boyd's biography. Gosse's books are yet to be given the digitised treatment that I've seen for so many other Victorian poets.

There is another afterlife for Emily. Just over two miles north, alongside the River Lea, the Unite union run a student accommodation called Emily Bowes Court. Taking her maiden name, the link to trade unionism is perhaps drawn from Emily's philanthropic work in the East End. The building is rigged to the earth like an external hard drive, painted in green and brown stripes, dropped onto the waste land beside the ancient river. Its 300 windows coruscating watery reflections. The Stansted Express stops outside.

Behind the cemetery, houselights are switched on. A motorbike revs: courier on dispatch. The storm has paused and now come the birds, singing the symphony of territory. The wind lifts its heels, runs for the trees. Ten minutes to closing. Time to move. And as I do, I practically run into Gosse's headstone. Nothing ornate: a functional slab, five feet high, falling forwards – by degrees – face first, towards the loam.

THE DUST OF
EMILY GOSSE,
WHO SLEPT IN JESUS
FEB 9TH, 1857,
WAITS HERE THE MORNING
OF THE
FIRST RESURRECTION

The Garden of Invisible Trees, 1977

'How do we know they're there?', he asked.

'I was told this is the place', she said.

'Is it related to that bollocks saying: "if a tree falls in an empty forest, can you hear it?"'

'It's: "If a tree falls in a forest and no one is around to hear it, does it make a sound?"'

'Same thing'.

'It's not a saying'.

'What is it then?'

'A thought experiment ... about perception'.

'So you brought me here for a thought experiment?'

'This is real, just try and listen ...'

Jason closed his eyes and listened. As he did, a lagoon opened in the ground of the forest and a thousand trees fractured its surface, a spartan battalion, linked branch-to-branch; a shoal of merlin, spearing the bottomless waters. There were two suns in the lake – one blurring the other – like Iron Age coins, spurned by a magnetic earth. Between the trees and the suns, a figure rose:

Hydromutter, goddess of the forest, unseen by man since the days before Christ. Trace stared, took a gasp of breath, stepping back as the goddess raised her wings and – like some vampire squid from the Midnight Zone – bared her jagged teeth:

'I can't hear anything...', Jason said frustratedly, opening his eyes with disappointment. 'Trace? … Trace!'

Trace was on the floor, lying on her back, frozen. Jason remembered that the nearest defibrillator was in Blandford Forum. He panic-checked his pockets for his phone, wolf-glaring at this land without 4G: 'This fucking … barren … shithole', he cried, holding Trace's head like a marrow, already relict in a previous Millennium.

Descendants of Nobody
— THOMAS WILLIAM ROBERTSON & DR ALEXANDER JAPP

When I first came up to London I had no thought of literature as a career. Indeed, I never have thought of it as a career, but only as a destiny.
ARTHUR MACHEN, *FAR OFF THINGS*

THOMAS WILLIAM ROBERTSON (1829-1871) was the grandson of a man who had published a book of verse under the name of 'Nobody'. Have I been handed another red herring? I arrive in the hour before closing, early April, and the temperature is rapidly dropping. The first midges of the season are cutting confused figures of eight. I walk up the path from Stamford Hill and spot a raw egg on the floor, cracked, lying next to the information sign for the Commonwealth war graves; the gaps in the earth absorb the albumen.

I'm here to find out if Robertson was a poet; his grave, apparently, states 'Dramatic Author'. Most poets I've met are dramatic authors, but did Robertson flex that drama in verse?

Spurred on by the recent finds – Newton, Conder and Gosse – my gut tells me that Abney Park will be the closest I've come to finding a great lost poet. This could be the place; the arboretum as outdoor library.

Born in Nottinghamshire in 1829, Robertson moved to London in his late teens to earn a living through writing and acting. His biographer Thomas Edgar Pemberton writes: 'The amount of work that he did there during his early struggling days was prodigious. In addition to writing and adapting plays, he contributed stories, essays, and verses to many magazines: dramatic criticisms to several newspapers: and ephemeral work to numerous comic journals.' Another of Abney Park's polymaths, or as he has been described, 'a theatrical hack-of-all-trades'.

His headstone won't be hard to find, I've been told: first turn from the entrance, visible path-side. This is the kind of can't-go-wrong instruction I've had before, ending in a meltdown under rhododendrons. In the trees above, green parakeets are maniacally impersonating themselves. A stranger bird soars over me, making the sound of an '80s ringtone; I look up, and see only a cross-shaped headstone, with one of its arms broken off. The structure floats in space like a lower case 't'.

After years of graft, Robertson was on the verge of giving

up when he stumbled into success. In 1865 his play *Society* was a big success for London's Prince of Wales theatre, leading him to write many more for the company. Robertson's plays are considered by theatre historians as having invented the modern era of stagecraft. He went on to write *Ours* (1866), *Caste* (1867) and *School* (1869) – all of them hits. When *Caste* was revived in 1897, George Bernard Shaw wrote: 'After years of sham heroics and superhuman balderdash, *Caste* delighted everyone by its freshness, its nature, its humanity.' Major praise, but for my purpose, these are not plays with any interest in the poetic. Their purpose is to delight with humorous, quick dialogue:

> NAOMI: [repeating] Go on, Bella. The Prince fell in love—
> CLARA: What is love?
> MILLY: You silly thing!
> TILLY: Such ignorance!
> KITTY: That stupid Clara!

I walk over ground that appears to have been dug by claws. A fox, perhaps, or maybe a dead poet, desperate for a second opinion. As I'm taking a closer look at the ground, a man and woman pass by, holding hands; one of them raises their united hands up – as one – to point out something in a tree. I look too but cannot see whatever it is they can see.

Robertson's plays dealt with social problems in straightforward language, being described by one critic as 'cup and saucer'. Robertson – reformed poet – found humour in poetry as an artform:

> BUNNYTHORNE: Thoughts in a coal-hole! I hate poetry – I consider it ungentlemanlike. There never used to be any poetry in my time.

One of Robertson's plays *My Lady Clara* (later renamed *Dreams*) took its name from Tennyson's poem 'Lady Clare'. But where are Robertson's own poems, the ones he wrote when he first arrived in London? The search sends me down another lockdown rabbit hole, but they have disintegrated under stage light, become fine dust in the fierce white spot of stronger ambitions.

A man flies at me on a travel bike – tiny wheels spinning – wearing a leather jacket. Lockdown hair stuffed into a helmet. I step aside, misreading a headstone as BLESSED ARE THOSE WHO DIE IN LONDON. Stone lilies explode from the ground, like flares sent up from a premature burial. When a man is tired of life, he dies in London.

Five years after Robertson's death, the *Hackney and*

Kingsland Gazette reported the landscape around his memorial like this: 'It is known as Road A; at the commencement is a fine specimen of the deciduous American oak, and a short distance on the left hand side is a modest tomb of a dear neighbour and public figure, whose comedies of 'Caste,' 'School,' 'Ours,' &c., have done so much to revive a taste for the pure English drama'.

His funeral brought a sell-out crowd of a thousand people, including the entire company of the Prince of Wales theatre. There would have been more, but there was a miscommunication about the time of the burial. No option for a Facebook refresh: print and be damned. The *Daily Telegraph & Courier* wrote:

> The assemblage, numerous and notable as it was, would have been doubtless infinitely larger had not some misapprehension arisen with regard to the day and hour fixed for the funeral. There were also conflicting claims which necessarily kept many away who would have been otherwise present.

The man who had always insisted on rehearsals and thorough attention to detail, found his final curtain call stalled by mismanagement. Death is a surrealist, spilling her cup into the saucer of realism every time.

Robertson's funeral took place on a bright February

morning, with a gentle wind. The sun was said to be at its brightest just as the earth was poured over the coffin. Tom Hood, his friend and executor – and fellow Magnificent Seven burial – was present, as was Marie Wilton, actor-manager of the theatre company, who placed the flowers on the coffin. The newspaper gave the full details of what is written on his memorial, which appears in front of me now; a high pedestal, like a tablet of camouflage – brown, green and white – its surface layer crumbling, with the text just about legible. The urn at the top is still half covered, and in the case of this writer who knew success – remains half full.

§

A few days later and the cemetery draws me back, this time on the hunt for Dr Alexander Japp (1837-1905), a poet described as 'protean' and 'many sided'. Japp's obituary in the *Dundee Courier*, from October 1905, describes him as 'a well-known literary man, and a voluminous author'. His friend Robert Louis Stevenson is a natural figure to emerge from my walks here, a writer of doubles and doppelgängers. Perhaps it was thinking about these connections which led to last night's dream, about a garden where I was employed as an amanuensis for a doppelgänger. Japp himself wrote under the cover of nom de plumes. As Machen observed,

Stoke Newington can be further understood through writers who focus on doubling: "I once knew a man,' said Perrott, 'who knew all about Stoke Newington; at least he ought to have known about it. He was a Poe enthusiast'. I don't know if Japp was a follower of Poe but he did further the modern Gothic through aiding the publication of Stevenson. Japp was also a wilful scatterer of his identity. I also sense a fire in this Scot, validated by reading this note that he placed before a sonnet sequence: 'To *some* of my "friends," who failed to acknowledge the free New Year's gift of my volume, or did so in merely perfunctory general terms'.

Japp isn't easy to locate here, but then why would anyone with so many aliases want to be found? The rainfall over the past week has muddied the paths; the ground gives no traction as I follow the map along Road B, towards the Boundary Path, passing infinite dead ends. Japp's pseudonyms include J.H. Alexander, H.A. Page and A.N. Mount Rose. There is something of Machen's world in Japp, a fringe figure of the London underworld.

This is the kind of writer I've found before in my journeys through the Magnificent Seven: bibliophiles resistant to daylight, anaemic, hunched over a creaking desk for days, dust settling on their shoulders. Sometimes they're found dead in that state: heart attack, physical shock at the cusp of literary enlightenment, never to be committed to paper. In Machen's novel *The Hill of*

Dreams (1907), Lucian Taylor devotes his life to this kind of obscurantism. Leaving Wales for the western fringes of London, Taylor spends his days between his desk – continuously writing the same paragraph with slight changes – and long walks in the rain, kicking around brickfield sites. Japp took a similar route. After finishing his degree, he moved to London, took a job as a journalist, and was drawn to the darker seams of the city, 'the lapsed masses and … criminals', as his obituary claims. Quartz retrieved from the city's dark matter.

A jogger pounds past; his feet, like heavy fish, slap against mud. Blackbirds and robins orchestrate the path before me. Squirrels with invisible thread knit the branches together. Then the garden gifts me a new discovery: the *sound* of squirrels. A duck-like, rattling lisp, calls from tree to tree.

'Dr Japp was many sided', the *Dundee Courier* goes on, 'in his literary productiveness, writing upon many subjects, though biography had for him great attractions'. Biographers are always subject to be less important as writers than those they write about, but here is the gamble: their work lasts in enduring footnotes of the fame they help perpetuate. Without Alexander Gilchrist – who died writing the one book he is known for – we would have far less understanding of William Blake. Japp's work on Robert Louis Stevenson contained personal letters from R.S.L. himself, and it was Japp who first helped to get *Treasure Island* into print, scooping up the first half of the manuscript after a visit to the ailing Scot and arranging for it to be serialised in a journal.

I follow the outer boundary of the cemetery, checking for a turn into the undergrowth that should be about here. Japp also wrote poetry criticism: his book *The Three Great Teachers of Our Time* (1865) evaluated the work of Carlyle, Ruskin and Tennyson. You can tell a lot about a poet from the things they say about other writers and Japp's refusal to make any all-encompassing claims is encouraging: 'Poetry is like life in this, that it eludes all attempts to close and fix it in definitions, and will not square itself off with theories, any more than the sea will remain at one level.'

I stop at a path, perhaps this is the one I should follow? But the landscape in front of me is bleak. A tree has forked its branches around a stone, claiming it, and an urn appears at my feet, separated from its pedestal. Is my life half-shrouded or half full? People are passing behind, as if to pull me back onto a straight path, away from death. A man in his 20s walks past, speaking into his phone: 'Cool, but before you go let me tell you this quick story...'. It is a story I'll never know. But what about Japp's story? Is there a path back towards readership?

Amidst his cavalcade of alter egos, Japp's poetry – like Robertson's – is not so easy to find. Another obituary, published in the *Montrose, Arbroath and Brecin Review* (6th October 1905) writes: 'His poems are scattered up and down the pages of magazines, though several of them have already found a deserved place in volumes of selected verse.' I check the British Library and a minor avalanche of titles caches into my screen. *Dramatic Pictures, English Rispetti, Sonnets and Other Verse* was published by Chatto & Windus – still a major poetry press today – in 1894. The book is dedicated to 'Friends in Edinburgh and round it' and is divided into 'Dramatic pictures', 'English Rispetti', 'Narrative and Lyrical', 'Sonnets' and 'Translations'; an ambitious sweep across poetic form, but how does it read, over a century later?

The dramatic pictures are all monologues, written with a balladeering impulse and little concern for psychological penetration. More Kipling than Browning, but unlike Kipling, Japp's rhythm is awkward, buckling under the weight of end-rhyme:

> But the wildest of adventures I had down in Mexico,
> Where the climate is the very worst that ever I did know.
> Ah! 'twas there I met the little girl that took my heart away
> All down by Yetchaphetel, where I found myself one day.

> ('Tim Jackson's Tale')

With a liquid ease, the sun slips out from behind a cloud: blue sky curled with cumulus. Then it goes again, and the wind picks up, pummelling the poplars. Weather changes intuition, and I find myself staring, as if waiting for a sign. In front of me is a granite obelisk, stone stench pipe, with angels appearing – like smoke – from the top.

Japp's 'Rispetti' have introduced me to a new form. It is always exciting to discover a new form; there is no reference to Rispetti in the National Poetry Library catalogue, which searches across a quarter of a million bibliographic records. Japp had discovered this form in the work of the poet Augusta Webster, whose words he included as a preface to his sequence: 'I cannot but feel pleasantly flattered that you have dedicated your Rispetti to me', Webster writes. 'Perhaps I deserve the honour, since I have been the person who "showed the way," as you say, to Rispetti in English, but you are very good to me in your verses bestowing it, and I thank you gladly.' Webster had discovered the form while travelling to Florence; she learned one of the poems by heart, translated it, and then began to write her own, which were published in *A Book of Rhyme* (1881). It is unusual for a male Victorian poet to show such a courtesy to a female one.

So what does a Rispetti involve? It is a Tuscan folk verse form, composed of eight hendecasyllabic (11-syllable) lines. The form has a set rhyme scheme, which in its first incarnation was ababababcc, but later mutated to a ccdd ending. Japp's Rispetti follow the latter form. In one sense, Rispetti are akin to the opening octet of a sonnet (without its closing six-line sestet), though Rispetti move the iambic pentameter of that form into the more difficult to handle, 11-syllable lines. At least they should. Japp relaxed the rules, often forming lines of ten syllables, and further relaxing the metrical stress within each metrical foot. As Gerard Manley Hopkins had demonstrated, there is no detriment to relaxing a form in this way, and Japp's lines are enjoyable to read. To test it out – and wake up my body – I read one of Japp's poems to the wind:

> SWEET heart of secret minstrelsy – how far
>   Thy golden notes, like lightnings in the dark,
> Flash full, ebullient, and no rivals mar
>   That music flooding all the moonlit park.
> Hold, hold, and overpower me not with pain
> Of very sweetness; in thy keen, full strain,
>   Notes touch me to the quick – so piercing clear,
>   I dream and think a long dead love is here.

> ('The Nightingale')

Abney's garden accepts the poem – the birds even strike up to sing along – but the ground does not open at my feet. It has, however, got me over the threshold of the path and into this dense, overgrown landscape. Fallen trees are everywhere. I step over one as I walk. Another has snapped in half, a casualty of Storm Dennis perhaps, broken before the pandemic began. This is the wilderness that civilisation tries to claim, out of respect for the dead, but nature won't have it. Highway Patrol gates have been placed along the path along with red and white hazard signs. Stand back. Death unfinished.

I hear two women pass, back on the path, banking in their walk 'allowance': 'The garden is completely covered with wild garlic!' one of them says. I've been dreaming gardens for months now and now other gardens are being gifted to me. Gardens on the wind. The Garden of Wild Garlic.

My map shows that Japp should be here; it's easy on paper. I walk sideways along a narrow path, feet angling for traction on the broken stones. The foliage parts and I gain a view of Bouverie Road, out across the perimeter wall.

I stare back into this unclaimed territory. The feel of earth under my feet; the crisp break of a stick. Early blossom and decay seem to compete for dominance, the new feeds on the old. I stand for a long time in this island of green: listening to sounds in the trees above. Then another conversation moves closer, or am I edging closer to it? Out beyond Japp, young women are talking on a bench, drinking from bottles of beer: 'His artwork is incredible', one says, 'super gothic'.

Japp was a naturalist, this comes through the poems: 'flowers, in truth, are hymns of nature'. Like Isabella Varley Banks, the lost garden of his books is slowly coming back to life through print-on-demand editions. Amazon lists over a dozen titles. After years in the wilderness, his volumes on De Quincey can be ordered for same day delivery. *Dramatic pictures: English Rispetti Sonnets and Other Verses* is available instantly on Kindle. Poems that were mole-blinded for decades now blink out – text twitching – backlit by Android.

I've been told by a few people that this part of the cemetery is a live cruising ground. A fallen tree, resting on two graves, forms a proscenium arch: a dappled and concealed enclave for quick contact. It is true. I look up from the graves to a shock flash of naked buttocks. A young man is in the process of dropping his shorts, jockstrap in a twist, emblazoned tulip. Spring air where sun has not shone; shots of adrenaline; human touch. Facemask in place. Love without kisses.

I've been swallowed in an ocean of holly, but now comes another surprise: Japp's headstone is there, in lime green, hidden at the base of a poplar. His name is down the rostrum of text, following those of family members:

ALSO TO THE MEMORY OF
ALEXANDER HAY JAPP LL.D
WHO DIED 29TH SEPTEMBER 1905
IN HIS 68TH YEAR
"DEATH IS BUT BIRTH IN OTHER REALMS MORE RARE
GLAD WELCOME WRAPT IN EVERY SAD ADIEU."

The man who came to London to stake his claim has found it; this is his spot in Abney's garden. His own piece of earth in the city of imagination.

The Garden of Doppelgangers, 0000

No one has my eye colour
The DNA in me is unique
I have a distinct attitude
Perspective separates me
My habits are my own
I am wise in a worldy way
Experience made me like this
Creativity is my lock and key
My passions get me out of bed
My humour bails me out
I have taste like no other
I communicate, like this
Only I could plant this garden

Visionary Musick

—— AN SOS FOR MARY HAYS

*I believe it is a rule that almost every literary career, certainly every
literary career which is to be concerned with the imaginative side of
literature, begins with the writing of verses.*

ARTHUR MACHEN, *FAR OFF THINGS*

COLOSSAL TRUMPETS PEEL INTO THE SKY. Stone tulips. Thousands
pass here every day, walking under their shadow. Phone calls
made. School reports. Last minute plans. Late for work. Look
up, citizens of London: the otherworld is spinning its disc above
your heads. I'm back at the gates, only this time the April sun is
searing like June. The buses are filling up again; shops opening for
business: cashflow. Through the gates, the cemetery is alive with
birdsong.

I have been given a link to a writer who might just turn
out to be a poet. Abney Park Cemetery Trust Coordinator, Haydn,
mentions the existence of Mary Hays (1759-1843), prolific prose
writer and friend of Mary Wollstonecraft: but did Hays write
poetry?

Mary Hays was born to Baptist parents and grew up south of the river, in Southwark. Her father died when he was just 40 and Hays was brought up by her mother. When she was 18, she met her first and most enduring love, John Eccles; he died of a fever during their passionate engagement, which was captured in their letters:

> Last night he came.—Good God, what a scene!—He held me in his arms—sobs stopt his voice—he trembled—changed hot and cold alternately—then broke from me—walked about the room, and lifted up his eyes to heaven in a speechless way! What could I do? I was softened beyond expression—I endeavoured to console him—promised never to be the wife of any other—pressed his hand to my heart—my lips to his forehead.

> (Mary Hays letter to Mrs Collier, July 29, 1779)

Hays' radical leaning was demonstrated in her early letters to Eccles: 'I fear I have too often swerved from the rules which [prudence] dictates … Why should we sacrifice sincerity to politeness?' (29th July 1779). Hays intuitively understood the injustice of Eccles having acquired the classical education which she was denied, leading her to ask him to be her 'monitor' rather than lover: 'to teach her what he knew as a man without using his knowledge to hurt her as a woman' (Gina Luria Walker).

Hays attended the New College in Hackney, the newest and most radical of the dissenting academies, where she heard speakers of 'Enlightened Dissent' preach, often inviting them to the Hays' home in Gainsford Street, near to the clatter and stench of the Thames.

Hays moved towards linguistic innovation in her letters to Eccles: 'I shall certainly tire you with my *scribbilation* – that last word is not in English I believe, but ladies have a right to coin you know, 'tis a privilege they have held since the creation'. Her letters also show how much poetry was already a part of her life, quoting Cowper, Dryden, Milton, Pope, Young and her neighbour here in Abney, Isaac Watts. When John Eccles wrote his own poems for her, Hays was able to accept them as love statements, but also to gently chide their quality: 'A very pretty fancy are these same verses of yours, – a little conceited though, I think, – but poetical licence extends very far'.

Victorian headstones employ poetic licence: I read it all around me. The subdued maiden, cradling a cross, on the pedestal of Henry and Alice Bone. The half-shrouded urn over Alexander Rose. The huge granite slab which denotes the burial ground of Robert Littler. Death's poetic licence extends to untruths: Edward Worral, whose headstone states was 'beloved by all'. The body remembered under the single name 'Patrick': 'to live in hearts we leave behind, is not to die'. Sometimes the licence is ditched for sheer poetry, as Frederick John Shirley's demonstrates: 'The spirit and the bride say come'. Headstones, however, should never leave room for misinterpretation, such as the statement on William "Willie" Chrees', which reads: 'sincerely regretted'.

Hays and Eccles could see each other across the street and would send signals to each other. Hays was at first refused permission to marry, but just as that permission was given, Eccles caught the fever that killed him. Once her grief had passed, his death created a loophole whereby she could live – not as a wife – but as a writer, reader and thinker.

Hays soon befriended Mary Wollstonecraft and William Godwin and moved to Hatton Garden to be near them. In fact, it was Hays who introduced them to each other, over tea, the future married couple finding 'friendship [melting] into love' (Godwin). Wollstonecraft offered comments on Hays' *Letters and Essays, Moral and Miscellaneous* (1793), writing notes in the margins with pencil, so that Hays could choose to 'adopt or erase … without much trouble' (Wollstonecraft, letter to Hays, November 25th 1792).

As I walk, my breathing suddenly feels laboured – I touch my mouth: facemask. Forgot to remove it. This appendage that was so strange – for so long – is now a fixture, an obsidian jawline. I check the nearest foliage for herbs; I could rip some out and stuff them inside, like a plague doctor.

Hays' published work aligned with Wollstonecraft's vision of equality for women. Hays wrote the obituary for the more famous author, which was published in the *Monthly Magazine*, as well as a memoir for her, published in the saliently titled *Annual Necrology*. Galvanised by *The Vindication of the Rights of Women*, Hays wrote the epic *Female Biography, containing the Memoirs of Illustrious and Celebrated Women of all Ages and Countries: Alphabetically Arranged* (1803), a book containing the 302 short biographies of female lives, written 'for women, and for scholars'. The book supplied Hays with sufficient royalties to buy a small house outside of London. Mary Shelley, Wollstonecraft and Godwin's daughter wrote to Hays describing her as one of those women 'whose talents do honour to our sex'.

A corvus shakes its death rattle above me, drawing me deeper into Abney's garden. I look up as I walk, reminded of a dream of a few nights back, which took place in a garden of hanging things. Strange creatures moved through the landscape as The Cure played a song (I realised later that I was dreaming a version of the video to their song 'The Hanging Garden'). I am in the right part of the cemetery, but where is the headstone I am looking for?

Hays would use her writing to expose the culture of rape, with her second novel *Victim of Prejudice* (1799) written 'to delineate the mischiefs that have ensued from the too great a stress placed on the reputation for chastity in woman'. The misogyny of the time can be seen in the acerbic responses from men to her work, with one of her books described as 'an abortion' and others attacking Hays' physical appearance. Men were made to sweat into their smoking jackets. Hays challenged the virginity taboo, deconstructing the social norm of 'respectability' which stated that women must be chaste in order to find employment. She tried to rationally appeal to the male tribe, writing *Appeal to the Men of Great Britain in Behalf of Women* (1798), but there were very few men who wanted to be appeased.

There are moments in Hays' political writing which synchronised with much later feminist figures, the move towards finding a 'Room of One's Own' for example. As she wrote to Godwin: 'I have been, in some measure, fortunate in the situation I have chosen, my apartments … are commodious, & the terms reasonable'. Hays sent a soundwave into the future, towards punk icons such as Poly Styrene, lead singer of the Punk band X-Ray Spex, who wrote against the plasticity of culture in 'Oh Bondage! Up Yours!' Hays wrote:

Of all bondage, mental bondage is surely the most fatal; the absurd despotism which has hitherto, with more than gothic barbarity, enslaved the female mind, the enervating and degrading systems of manners by which the understandings of women have been chained down to frivolity and trifles, have increased the general tide of effeminacy and corruption.

(*Letters and Essays, Moral and Miscellaneous*, 1793)

And just as Poly Styrene would later express, Hays was appalled by the vacuousness of fashion: 'To conform to the perpetual fluctuation of fashion', Hays writes, 'requires almost their whole time and attention, and leaves little leisure for intellectual improvement'. The range of subjects that Hays covered shows a facility for thinking across binaries; she imbricates themes as diverse as oratory, civil liberty, authority and materialism. She was driven by 'the satisfaction in the idea of *being free* … a desire of strengthening my mind by standing alone' (Letter from Hays to Godwin).

I have been standing at the end of the Yew Walk for too long, glancing up from the map – and back – like a heron in cement. I solicit help and text a Trust Coordinator. SOS Heritage.

Hays lies somewhere here, alone; there is no one else in her grave. Here is a poet who had circulated amongst the poets of the time. She met Robert Southey and Coleridge, and became friends with an unstable versifier called Charles Lloyd, who mocked her (Lloyd would later be confined to an asylum and turned up on De Quincey's doorstep claiming to be the devil). The risk of physical and verbal assault, prejudiced reviews of her work, the ridicule of 'friends' – it would have been so easy for Hays to retreat, to recoil from public life, but she persevered: this was her vocation. She leaned into the headwind, writing until death.

The Trust Coordinator appears on the Yew Walk. She points out what was in front of me all along. Hays' headstone is textless, an oddity; it has a Gothic turret on each side and a white, shaley texture.

It is Hays' prose which attract scholarly attention today. Her novel *Memoirs of Emma Courtney* (1796) was radical, containing techniques which experimental writers still use today. The book absorbed trends such as Wollstonecraft's new journalism, along with Hays' unreciprocated letters to William Frend, who had declined her offer of a romantic relationship. Controversy followed its publication: lambchop sideburns grilling on apoplectic faces. Robert Southey said the work was 'an uncommon novel, much praised and much abused'. Its brilliance is in combining fiction with real events – and real letters – thereby anticipating the birth of Modernism by 100 years.

But Hays' poems have slipped from history, like the text on her headstone – words erased by time – type replaced with a series of blotches: white spectres and purple scars. I try to make out something from the surface, a word – even a letter – but the centuries have done their editing. I lean in, across the vines, and read all that remains:

MARY H   Y

'Invocation to the Nightingale' was published in 1781, in *The Lady's Poetical Magazine, or, Beauties of English Poetry*. Hays used a pseudonym which she would also make use of in her prose work: 'Eusebia', the Greek goddess of piety. It is a misguiding pseudonym – perhaps used ironically – given the radicalness of her later work:

Invocation to the Nightingale

Wand'ring o'er the dewy meadow,
    Oft at ev'ning hour I go;
Fondly courting Philomela's
    Sympathetick plaints of woe.

Sometimes, hush'd in still attention,

Leaning pensive o'er a stile,
Fancy bids her sound delusive
    Lull the yielding sense awhile.

Soft the visionary musick,
    Rising floats upon the gale:
Now it sinks in strains more languid,
    Dying o'er the distant vale

Starting from the dream of fancy,
    Nought my list'ning ears invade,
Save the hum of falling waters,
    Save the rustling aspin-shade.

'Little songstress, soothe my sorrows,
    'Wrap my soul in softest airs;'
'Such as erst, in Lydian measures,
    'Charm'd the Grecian hero's cares. […]

Vain, alas! my Invocation,
    Vain the pleadings of the muse!
Wrapp'd in silent shades, the charmer
    Doth her tuneful lay refuse.

Clouds obscure deform the aether,

Rising damps involve the plain;
Pensively I hasten homeward,
    To avoid the coming rain.

Had John Keats read this poem in his youth, taking it as a source for 'Ode to a Nightingale'? The concept of both poems is similar, drawing on Greek references. In the fifth stanza, Hays' poem switches its focus to direct conversation with the bird, whereas Keats cuts out any sense of preamble, beginning in the midst of his 'drowsy numbness'. There is a connection with reality in Hays' poem that Keats is less interested in; he writes instead from the murkiness of imagined drug use and self-obsession, pushing towards what Freud called the 'death drive'. Hays' poem was written before the advancements of Romanticism – it conforms to the Augustan beat – but there are moments which prefigure the synaesthetic compression of Keats: 'Fancy bids her sound delusive / Lull the yielding sense awhile'. Undercutting the lack of self-care in Keats, Hays' ends with good common sense – the speaker returning home to avoid the rain.

I try and glean more text on the worn headstone: nothing. 'Coco!' a woman shouts – seeking a pet or a hot beverage – and a flagging terrier appears from a bush, panting, its tongue like carpaccio.

Hays' 'Ode to Her Bullfinch' is a conversational lyric, more limber in form, using the heptasyllable (seven syllable line). The poem addresses the less poetic bullfinch, who is under attack from 'a wily fowler' – symbolic, perhaps, of incumbent male power:

Little wanton flutt'rer, say
Whither wou'dst thou wing thy way?
Why those airy circles make,
All untry'd the thorny brake?
Various dangers lurking lie
In the guise of liberty;
See the wily fowler laid
Close beneath the hawthorn shade;
Mark his tyrannous intent,
Full on schemes of murder bent; [...]

Lest the school-boy's truant eye
Shou'd thy tender young descry;
Lest the ruder vernal storm
Shou'd thy little nest deform,
Hither then, thou wanton, fly,
Bless thy soft captivity;
And lull with notes of soothing sound
The pangs which do my bosom wound.

Ellen Moody writes that in Hays' poems 'small animals are caged, tortured, killed or just fail to survive in a harsh natural world'. Hays refuses to let this pass in silence. The poem tells us that the bullfinch is female, the mother of chicks, whom the speaker expresses concern that a schoolboy might 'thy tender young descry'. If male oppression is latent, the speaker of the poem offers a 'bosom' in which the birds can 'safely lie'. The form of the poem captures urgency, with each line ending with a resounding stressed word. Reading the poem out loud gives a sense of being rushed, harassed – the result of fear and resistance.

Birdsong in Abney is war music and coded information; the ongoing, diurnal quest for survival. Face, beak, claws. On the other side of Hays' headstone, a man speaks into his phone: 'Have a great day!' His voice lost in the vines.

Hays had further afterlife in the Romantic era, with Charles Lamb attacking her in a letter to another woman:

G— forbid that I should
pass my days
with Miss Hays

(Charles Lamb letter to Matilda Betham, Sep 27, 1811).

Coleridge derided her cruelly as 'a thing ugly & petticoated'. This is the other side of the imaginative flights of Romanticism: male spite. Hays knew the terrain she was writing in; it was what drove her.

A robin perches on a holly tree in front of me. It sits like a sherry flute, body stock still, while its head absorbs the trembling world around it. The nib of its face writing the landscape.

Hays' poems were for a long time hard to find. 'Ah! let not hope fallacious, airy, wild' was included in the anthology *A Century of Sonnets: The Romantic-Era Revival, 1750-1850*. In 2002, Philippa Gregory, Hays' great-great-great-great grandniece, adapted the poet's love letters for an episode of BBC Radio 4's 'Woman's Hour'. This was followed two years later by the publication of Hays' letters. But it is her fiction that is still in print with a big publisher, and she remains best known for her alliance and friendship with the Wollstonecraft circle. Her poems have fallen down the cracks. It is time for a reappraisal, I think, looking at the ground beneath her headstone, where English ivy and raspberry brambles compete for the fiefdom. The headstone will be completely covered by the end of the summer.

Mary Hays died quite suddenly in 1843, after a short illness. Her brother's letter to Henry Crabb Robinson (an important correspondent with Blake) is an eldritch squib, capturing the Victorian confusion around death: 'my Sister Mary … rising in her bed yesterday morning to prepare breakfast and then falling back, without even a sigh, upon her pillow, became a Corpse. May my last end be like hers.' Hays had explicitly stated that she wished to be buried at 'the cemetery at Newington'. There was a small gathering of men at her funeral; they formed a broken ring around the grave.

'I sought', she once wrote to Crabb Robinson – who stood with her brothers as the coffin was lowered – 'and made myself an extraordinary destiny'.

The Garden of Hanging Things, 2054

— And you say this music video gives a clue to the portal?

— Yes, it was conceived by The Cure to be so.

— And no one cracked the code while the band were alive?

— No, they were sworn to secrecy, never to speak of it in their lifetime.

The video starts: screen washed in swamp green. Backdrop of classical statues. Robert Smith, hair thatched: flat eyrie waiting for an eagle to perch. Site of a lake. Central island of sapling trees.

Then the band appear with instruments: backlit by colonnades and a statue of a naked nymph. They begin to play, led by the bass.

— The answer is in the statues then?

— No, listen to the words ...

— 'Jump, out of time ...'

— Beneath the band, are the dead buried there?

— All of our energies must be driven in that direction ...

– Where are these Gardens?

– York House, Twickenham.

– Beneath the Sunken Lawn, often used for open air summer shows, there is an attrition of bodies, retrieved one night from the nearby St Mary's churchyard. The Poet Alexander Pope, and Tennyson's son Hallam, are amongst them.

– And The Cure knew this, but could not speak?

– That is what we must prove ...

The video continues: statues replicate on the lawn. Stone lions bookend the island of trees. Smoke blows across the screen, now washed in purple. The band wear masks. Close up of a fish-head statue. Obsidian armadillo walks across the lawn. Statues replicate: vines grow over them. Screen washed in red. Full moon. A stooped man in furs retreats behind a rock. Statues of horses. Screen washed in blue.

Then the band and the statues disappear. Just the Hanging Garden remains.

Beneath the garden: London's transient dead.

Bones Around the Mutterkreuz

— ALICE R. CRON & WILLIAM HONE

Here was I well equipped with long-gathered material for a sermon on
the great text that there is wonder in everything and everywhere, wonder
above all in this great town that has grown so vast that no man can know
it, nay, nor even begin to know it!

ARTHUR MACHEN, *THE LONDON ADVENTURE*

I STOP TO PAUSE, OVERWHELMED by the discoveries I've made.
Was Mary Hays the great lost poet I'm looking for? Not quite,
but she was extremely talented and her life story is one that I'm
glad to have traced back to her grave. Encouraged by this, I have
discovered links to two more poets: a female war poet called Alice
R. Cron (1859-1935) and an author and campaigner for civil
liberties, who happened to write poetry: William Hone (1780-
1842).

Alice Cron's headstone reads: WRITER AND POETESS.
She is buried with her husband James, who died four years later.
They share a narrow mound of earth, adjacent to the closed
catacombs and aligned with the war memorial.

Cron was recently found by Alison Paler and other volunteers, raising excitement that a female war poet – of which there are few – is buried in Abney Park. Cron is another of Abney's pathside burials, the extent of which is a phenomenon in my journey around the Magnificent Seven.

A kneeling angel can be seen, in relief, on Cron's headstone, a trompe-l'œil; the stone figure tends to real ivy. There is also a short poem:

> Farewell in hope and love
> In fate and peace and prayer
> Till we whose home is ours above
> Unite us there.

In March 2018 I gave a performance in Abney Park's chapel, the thaw yet to pass – the audience perched in the dark – with volunteers handing out blankets to stop them slipping away with the dead. At the time, Cron was unknown to me. The next day, one of the volunteers sent me an email, explaining that she had found Alice Cron's headstone the week before. There was a buzz among the staff. Their Abney Unearthed project was working, and here was the evidence: a female war poet brought to light.

To the light, but few known facts glint. Cron was born

Alice Rebecca Taylor in Hackney in 1859, the first of five siblings. In 1880 she married James Philip Cron, a German glove maker; a decade later and the couple had moved from Hackney to Stoke Newington. In 1891 they lived on Heathland Road and by 1911 they were living at Amhurst Park, Stamford Hill, on the north side of the cemetery. They later returned to Hackney, their last known address.

Hackney had one of the largest populations of Germans in the UK, and in 1845 the German Hospital was built to serve this community. The German Hospital takes over my thoughts for a while, a red-brick enclave that is now Grade II listed and used for housing. The hospital survived two world wars, courting the bombs dropped from its motherland. The staff in the hospital were interned in World War Two. Stoke Newington was badly damaged in the Blitz, as documented in *Bomb Damage Maps, 1939-45*: 'Approximately 12 houses were destroyed, 140 seriously damaged, 300 affected. A report at 6 p.m. on 8 January [1941] records that ten people were killed, 18 seriously injured and 29 slightly injured. About 200 people were rendered homeless.'

On the western side of the cemetery, the houses on Bouverie Road were damaged beyond repair and those forming the perimeter of the grounds were 'seriously damaged – repairable at cost'. One hundred and fifty-four people died in the bombing of nearby Coronation Mansions, they were trapped in the underground shelter as water and effluent poured in. Twenty-six of them were never identified. Bridget Penney describes the Abney House corner of the cemetery as 'a strange confused mixture of tomb stones, several of which were flattened or badly damaged by a bomb'. Parts of Defoe Road experienced total destruction. At the epicentre of the cemetery, the chapel remained undamaged; seen from a bomber, the chapel would have appeared as a replica of the German Mother Cross (Mutterkreuz): a stranded crucifix.

Cron never published a complete collection but she did appear in the anthology *A Hundred Best Poems* (1916). Her poem 'The Call of the King' is a patriotic rallying cry for the British troops fighting in France:

HURRAH ! for the men who are fighting to-day!
 Those heroes undaunted and brave,
Who go forth in thousands with hearts bright and gay,
 The honour of England to save !
No fear of the foe — whose numbers so vast —
 Places ours as one against ten.
The call of their King, as it did in the past,
 Suffices for our gallant men.

Hurrah ! then for England ! that land in the sea!

> Whose sailors are always on guard ;
> Whose soldiers are fighting three countries to free
> From the Kaiser's loving regard.
> So Bravo ! dear Belgium ! Hurrah for La France !
> But the loudest Hurrah ! of all
> For Britons ! — Welsh, Irish and Scotch who advance
> To answer their country's first call.

The poem is problematic. It has an awkward musicality, with the penultimate line forgetting its own metrical pacing, cramming in the names of UK countries: 'Welsh, Irish and Scotch who advance / To answer their country's first call.' Excitable energy flies backwards down the trumpet.

There are echoes in Cron's work of the more famous Jessie Pope, who wrote poems to encourage children to enlist before they received a coward's 'white feather'. As the war went on, and the mood of the nation changed, the reality of trench warfare could be seen in the poems of Wilfred Owen and Siegfried Sassoon. Owen wrote his vivid, phantasmagoric 'Dulce et Decorum Est' directly for Pope:

> If you could hear, at every jolt, the blood
> Come gargling from the froth-corrupted lungs,
> Obscene as cancer, bitter as the cud

Of vile, incurable sores on innocent tongues,—
My friend, you would not tell with such high zest
To children ardent for some desperate glory,
The old Lie: *Dulce et decorum est*
Pro patria mori.

It is sweet and fitting to die for one's country. Owen would have taken the same view of Cron's poem, writing in the Preface he wrote for a book that he would never see published: 'This book is not about heroes. English poetry is not yet fit to speak of them ... All a poet can do today is warn. That is why the true Poets must be truthful.'

The First World War prompted severe hate attacks on the 50,000 plus German population living in Great Britain, many of whom had set up small businesses such as barbers and bakers – or glove-makers, in the case of Cron's husband. As an established married couple, contributing to society, and feeling part of an integrated community, Alice and James had no way of being prepared for the xenophobia that followed the outbreak of war. The Aliens Restriction Act limited Germans from moving more than five miles; German newspapers and clubs were closed with many properties confiscated without compensation; and all males between the age of 17 and 55 were interred in camps.

Rumours began to circulate that there was a German 'hidden hand' (a worrying phrase for a maker of gloves) controlling Britain and preventing British victory. This led the Royal Family to change their name from Saxe-Coburg-Gotha to Windsor, and to widespread riots in which nearly 2,000 German properties in London were plundered and destroyed. By the end of the war, the number of Germans in the UK had halved, to just over 20,000. These facts change my initial reading of Cron's poem, which I now begin to see as her own weapon of deflection, an attempt to do something to protect herself – and her husband – from the threat of violence. There is a great deal of specificity in the poem, not only for 'The call of their King', but also against 'the Kaiser's *loving regard*'. Poetry becomes a tool in a personal campaign, levied against internal British prejudice, skilfully engineered through gushing patriotism. In this reading, the style of the poem is key: message must take dominance over form or stylistic invention – the poem cannot afford to miss the zeitgeist.

I also have a copy of Cron's poem 'The Flowering Month of May', which confirms that 'The Call of the King' was not deliberately badly written, as this second poem contains several of the same awkward elements. The poem reveals Cron to be another of Abney's nature lovers:

'Oh! Come and see the flowers in my garden!
     Their colours are so wonderful just now
With Irises in mauve, and white and yellow,
     And Lilics full in bloom upon the bough. [...]

Then Rhododendrons, Peonies, Clematis –
     In white and scarlet, purple 'gainst the wall
With Cherry Blossoms pink, and bright Laburnum
     And God's blue heaven a-shining over all!'

The colour purple – 'Irises in mauve' – is following me again. The sun scatters coins over Cron's grave as I consider her poem – metrically uneven as any herbarium – as a statement on Abney Park's arboretum, speaking for the current nation of lockdown nature lovers.

Cron is a long way from the poet I have set out to find – a Hopkins or a Dickinson – but she has taken me further into Abney's transient garden. I've waited so long to be here, in this garden that can only be experienced in the present moment. The life of a poet can do that too.

§

I try again with William Hone. Each poet's work starts a new path towards unexpected connections and chance encounters, this is how all libraries work and Abney Park is no exception. Hone is buried more closely to the chapel, in another of the four islands that surround it. Hone was once described as the most famous man in Britain but died virtually unknown; his remains are now lying in the shadow of a Celtic cross. He was a burly man with a hood of darkness above his eyes; wayward with money, he was always scheming towards his next – usually failed – venture. I've arranged to meet Zachariah Young, Trust Coordinator, and to be filmed reading one of Hone's parodies – a small offering towards the literary afterlife. Our decision to foreground a dead poet through digital technology might have led to my latest strange dream in which a I was experiencing a future garden landscape through a virtual reality headset. Zombies were out to get me.

'I derived a love for quiet and the country', Hone wrote, 'which has yearned in me throughout life'. Like Machen, he was drawn to the fringes of London: to Islington, Highgate, Hampstead and, presumably, the village he is buried in, Stoke Newington. After failing in a savings bank venture, then a printing shop, Hone became notorious for an 1817 court case in which he stood accused of criminal libel for creating prints that were harmful to public morals. His works of parody were at the centre of the controversy, particularly his distortion of the Lord's Prayer

('O House of Lords, hereditary legislators, have mercy upon us, pension-paying subjects'). Hone's appearances in court badly damaged his health, but his refusal to lie down was a landmark for freedom of the press in this country. His victory – which required defending himself for up to seven hours a day – has led to him being called the 'father of modern media'. Up until his court case, the government could decide what constituted 'dangerous' works, and juries were usually composed of pre-selected men who were seen as 'upstanding' citizens. Ben Wilson argues that 'His career showed that laughter had a *legitimate* political role; it was a fundamental freedom for a people shackled by repressive laws'. When Hone was acquitted he was met with huge supportive crowds outside of court.

It was a short-lived period of respite; in 1826 he was imprisoned again, this time due to the inability to pay debts owing on his journal the *Every-day Book*. One reason for the project failing was that Hone was trying to keep the cost down for families who would otherwise struggle to afford the publication.

Throughout his life, Hone was friends with poets, including Charles Lamb (who Hone called the only man who knew him intimately), William Hazlitt, Robert Southey and Leigh Hunt. Hone lived on the fringes of Romanticism but was more grounded in political reality than most of the poets. When

Hone was on trial, Coleridge argued for the necessity of saving him in order to save English law. It is clear to see why poets were drawn to him; he was a man who stood up to authority, deriving his creative work from the circulation of political and artistic ideas. Like so many poets, Hone lived under a lifelong depression – or Hypochondria as he called it, in the popular expression – believing in laughter as one of the few antidotes to the black dog.

Zach appears in a long coat; he is a part of a new generation inspired by London's Victorian cemeteries and with an innate understanding of their significance. As he sets up the camera, I prepare to read Hone's parody by taking deep lungfuls of air. It will be needed in order deliver *The Political House that Jack Built* (1819), with its racing rhythm of the nursery rhyme. The original publication was illustrated by George Cruikshank, detailing a bloated Prince Regent (future George IV), who had jumped to the defence of the Manchester Yeomanry Cavalry after they had reaped carnage on innocent bystanders in Manchester. At the time of the Regent's letter of approval, he was sitting on a Royal Yacht, the sun on his back. Hone later wrote a report detailing the people who died, including women and a child.

Zach places the tripod, raises a hand in the air, and standing alongside Hone's headstone, I step into the poem:

This is THE MAN–all shaven and shorn,
All cover'd with Orders–and all forlorn;
THE DANDY OF SIXTY,
         who bows with a grace,
And has *taste* in wigs, collars,
            cuirasses and lace;
Who, to tricksters, and fools,
           leaves the State and its treasure,
And, when Britain's in tears,
         sails about at his pleasure

As we walk away from Hone, Zach on his way back to the cemetery office, I pass two men on a bench, talking: 'Middle class people getting arrested by the police?' one of them asks, 'Can they not think of something else? … Honestly though, my opinion is that I don't give a shit'. Political mismanagement never ceases – it circulates like bad air. Hone *did* give a shit and his parodies showed that poetry was a way of doing something about it. His book reached a wide public, going into 54 editions and selling over 100,000 copies.

In the last years of his life, Hone became a follower of Thomas Binney (1798-1874), buried here in 1874 with a funeral procession of 5,000 people; Binney's hymn 'Eternal Light' has also been presented as a poem in anthologies such as *The Sacred*

Poets of the Nineteenth Century (1907):

> The spirits that surround Thy throne
>   May bear the burning bliss;
> But that is surely theirs alone,
> Since they have never, never known
>   A fallen world like this.

'A fallen world like this': who saw this year of lockdown coming? I was in Munich as it unravelled, taking part in a festival of concrete poetry, facing the threat of cancelled flights: all that was solid melted into airspace.

The network grows: I find that Hone was also acquainted with Josiah Conder, working as his assistant for *The Patriot*. He had always been a Christian, but Hone experienced a conversion to a deeper piety which led him to renege on his earlier political work. *The Patriot* railed against the requirement for dissenting chapels to pay tithes to the Anglican mothership, and all of Hone's endeavours became aligned with this aim. This work was far from what Hone had known in his dynamic younger years; his role simply involved assembling facts from newspapers, to help Conder in the argument for reform. To limit the commuting time, Hone would sleep at the office, wake at seven, and work until midnight. Ben Wilson describes how one morning in 1837 Hone work up in the office, felt too ill to work, and experienced the first of a series of strokes. It was to this end that Hone used his later poetry; one day he tore a poem from the flyleaf of a bible – in itself a borderline heresy – and presented it to the Reverend Thomas Waffles, saying: 'take this as evidence and memorial of the change':

"Lines Written before breakfast, 3rd June 1834, the anniversary of my Birth Day in 1780"

"The proudest heart that ever beat
   "Hath been subdued in me;
"The wildest will that ever rose,
"To scorn Thy cause, and aid Thy foes,
   "Is quell'd, my God, by Thee.

"Thy will, and not my will be done;
   "My heart be ever Thine;
"Confessing Thee, the mighty Word,
"I hail Thee Christ, my God, my Lord,
   "And make Thy name my sign.

W. HONE.

This is a poem of personal ardency and I like how the last line conflates language with physicality: logos into sign. It captured Hone's regret at the end of his life, for what he saw as the squandering of happiness through a drive for knowledge: 'Sometimes I wished that I, too', he wrote, 'had been ignorant – ignorant of the book which had caused me to doubt, and to believe that death was annihilation. I began to question whether my knowledge was of any use. It gave liberty to do as I would, but not the power.' This is a reminder of the important of balance in a writer's life; not writing enough can bring regrets, but so can working too hard at the expense of other forms of happiness.

I have circled back on myself and am looking again at Hone's headstone. Charles Dickens was at Hone's funeral, later writing at length about it, describing the disconnection between Hone's weeping family – his widow and seven children – and the wider group of mourners who stood aside from them, calmly talking. Dickens had to fight back the laughter in observing George Cruikshank's appearance. 'Enormous whiskers', Dickens wrote, 'which straggle all down his throat in such weather, and stick out in front of him, like a partially unravelled bird's-nest'. Not every poet has a Dickensian account of their funeral. It was the send-off Hone deserved, and he would have approved of the laughter, especially on a day which Dickens described as 'muddy, foggy, wet, dark, cold and unutterably wretched in every possible respect … a scene of mingled comicality and seriousness … which has choked me at dinner ever since'. In 1864, Hone's wife Sarah was buried alongside him.

'A walk out of London', Hone once wrote, 'is, to me, an event'. I have already walked away from his headstone, taking him at his word.

The Garden of Virtual Reality, 2389

I carry a garden in a VR headset --- when I turn my head the
garden turns --- how can a garden turn? --- the headset must be
out-of-synch --- can I return it to the VR Corp? --- If only I could
leave this room --- I walk with my spine arched --- even though
I am flying --- then the zombies appear --- pale cadavers without
heads --- you know the sort --- they're coming from every angle
imaginable --- even the lake --- the deep black lake where children
wail --- the zombies multiply like carousel attendants --- the only
escape is *through* them --- marching into the forest --- things are
quiet for a while --- should I say Hello to Pennywise? --- perhaps
now --- do I want a balloon? --- yes, like a manatee wants a plug
in its spout --- now we're really gaming --- which is to say living
--- the garden has a cave --- inside is a Cyclops called Somebody
--- he wants to get me drunk --- but I don't drink --- so I walk
instead into a bowling green --- at the centre is the Lord Mayor
--- offering a free navel to anyone who queues --- this is the centre
of the garden --- where the truth becomes obvious --- generative
--- there you can look ahead --- with a crooked neck --- into the
world's absence

Dragged by an Alien Force

—— REVEREND THOMAS TOKE LYNCH

> *The unknown world is, in truth, about us everywhere, everywhere near to our feet; the thinnest veil separates us from it, the door in the wall of the next street communicates with it.*
>
> ARTHUR MACHEN, *THE LONDON ADVENTURE*

THE SPRING HAS GONE BACKWARDS, high pressure clearing the night sky, reducing the temperature to zero. The cemetery is deserted. I am surrounded by mausolea – a stone city sculpted from underground geology and re-hewn into memorials for the dead. I'm reminded of Machen's description of old London: 'the hand of man has so worked upon these rough masses, has so grouped them and carved them and carried them towards the skies, that you see the miracle of the dead raised to life, of the dull and shapeless mass informed with the living spirit'.

I am here to find a poet of the living spirit, one who wrote through physical pain and that rare phenomenon: a poetry controversy. The Reverend Thomas Toke Lynch (1818-1871) officiated at Mornington Church on Hampstead Road, where his own funeral service was held. The *Leeds Mercury* described the transition of the congregation to the cemetery: 'At the close of the service in the church a procession of between twenty and thirty carriages proceeded to Abney Park, where there was a considerable concourse of persons around the grave. Here, in a consequence of a shower of rain, the service was very brief.'

From the Stamford Hill side entrance, I head for his headstone, a stone bookmark on London's surface. I pass some Spanish bluebells – also known as wood hyacinth – drooping in the breeze.

Lynch is another of Abney's nonconformist preachers. He also wrote on the Millennium but his thoughts were less crystallised than Newton's, with Lynch's view of the Second Coming being full of energy and future hope: 'All spiritual men that we have ever read or conversed with, who have studied the Book of Revelation, have agreed, different as their interpretation of texts has been, that the study is one of extreme interest and of great moral worth, because it has buoyed up the best hopes of the soul ... Believe then in the Millenium as a great and good time coming' (from *The Mornington Lecture: Thursday Evening Addresses*). One of Lynch's poems envisages the Second Coming as a past event:

With many a swift and crashing stroke
   From clouds, the frigates of the sky,
Huge solemn-sailing clouds, there broke
   Victorious bursts of energy …

One general pleasure of release
   Pervades today the earth and sky ;
Bright quiet clouds, like ships of peace,
   The airy ocean beautify

   (from *The Rivulet* CLXIII)

Unlike some of the poets I've discovered in the Magnificent Seven, Lynch's prose does not steal the light from his poetry. What is crystallised here becomes slack and verbose in prose. 'THIS Tract though brief is comprehensive', he writes in his book *Among Transgressors* (1860), 'But then, though comprehensive, it is brief', sounding like a pastiche of Shakespeare's Polonius. It is the writing style of an author writing to fill the space of a weekly lecture slot – a bit of chiasmus doubles the word count.

   Lynch suffered ill health during his life, his friend Dr Samuel Cox described the conditions through which the Reverend tried to write:

Hardly was he seated at his desk before he was assailed by the rending, suffocating pangs of his cruel disease (*Angina pectoris*). As the work went on, the anguish grew, until the intolerable agony compelled him to fling himself on the floor, where he lay patiently and steadfastly enduring the pressure of his great pain. No sooner was the fierce spasm past than he rose, seated himself once more at his desk, and resumed his labour till seized by another intolerable spasm ... his handwriting, ordinarily so neat and regular, grows large, straggles wildly across or down the page, and looks as though his hand must have been jerked and dragged by an alien force.

Victorian poets wrote against many factors; not only against the risk of silence, but in this case, against the body itself, a reminder that writing is always a physical act. Writing becomes an alien force, a form of possession that throws the corpus to the floor. Against this, Lynch wrote with wild scrawls – waiting for the pain to pass in order to complete his art – eventually publishing 12 books. I wonder if this image of Lynch at his writing desk led to my latest dream, which involved an old house, a butler and a vision of a visionary garden involving two white chairs? Dead poets enter via Beulah, Blake's name for the subconscious that connects poetry with dreams.

The outer boundary of the cemetery is deserted today; a lone man walking, staring at the floor with a facemask mandible.

Every headstone vies for attention: James Alfred Spring, 'who died suddenly' on December 29th 1881. Then come the Ponders family, their surname saying something about the eternity of death. The grave of Anne Oake, with its missing lead type; it forms a broken missive from the dead, a disintegrating visual poem. It reads like a page from Wyndham Lewis's *Blast*, time as master of the art of spacing:

ANNE OAKE
I D A ST
Y   TH

        UD S   *IR*
    N   E BY   Y   D
    T   SHO   AI
D   COUL   M

A SO   EAR   L IT LE ARTHUR,
WHO DIED   UNE 30T
LD   2 MONTHS &   DAYS

I continue towards Lynch, another of Abney's hymnologists, edging into the hinterlands of poetry. He wrote that his poems 'are adapted for song as well as for perusal, hymns for both heart and voice'. This seems like an unlikely basis for a controversy, but his book *The Rivulet: a Contribution to Sacred Song* (1855), was the source for a fierce debate. The editor of the *Morning Advertiser* lambasted the work, writing that 'there was not one particle of vital religion or Evangelical piety in the book, that nearly the whole of his hymns might have been written by a Deist, and a very large portion might be sung by a congregation of Freethinkers.' Many church magazines followed in their critiques, with John Campbell of the British Banner and *Christian Witness* slating the text as 'miserable garbage'.

Lynch seemed to enjoy the controversy, which allowed his work to reach a larger readership. The current hymnology blog, 'Conjubilant with Song', writes: 'The resulting furore eventually threatened the very existence of the Congregational Union, a federation of Nonconformist and Congregational churches in England and Wales. The organization was careful never to endorse the use of the collection, which had so divided its members.' Alfred Miles describes how this controversy ran on: 'The strife was fierce and long, and drew to both sides many combatants beyond those first engaged'. On the side against Lynch was the 'Prince of Preachers', Charles Spurgeon, to whom Lynch responded with wordplay: 'We must conquer our foes by suffering them to crucify us, rather than by threatening them with crucifixion'. In the British

Library's 3rd edition of *The Rivulet* someone has defaced the text, perhaps in itself showing a continuation of the controversy well into the 20th century; one of Lynch's lines has been altered by a reader, who has crossed out the word 'work' and replaced it with 'lurk'.

Standing here and thinking about Lynch's *The Rivulet*, I have a moment of awareness of being *here*, feeling alive in the cemetery after a year of wall-staring; it is energising to be back in the city, with the pull of the old Hackney Brook under my feet – one of the city's many hidden waterways – once racing towards the pulmonary artery of the Lea. 'The River of Song makes glad the City of God', Lynch writes, 'and many who are weary and athirst as they pass through field or through desert, travelling towards the City, if they but drink of a brook by the way, can go on that way rejoicing'. Abney Park Cemetery is its own city of language, a stone library, and it occurs to me now how the past year has shifted the English language; we will never hear 'lockdown', 'facemask' or 'bubble' in the same way again. This altering of language changes how we read historic works too, such as poem CLVII from *The Rivulet*:

"A bubble I would be," says one;
"O, let me perish in the sun,

As brightly end as I begun!
It is not nothingness I shun,
For dark the course that I must run,
No prize can at the end be won."

Lynch's best poems are so of the moment, written with an immediacy for sound and thing and life, that it's impossible not to feel that joy transcend through the page to this moment – over 150 years after its first publication. The sequence reads like a jubilant version of Tennyson's *In Memoriam*, with Lynch's love for nature stirring within his body; nerves and senses compelling his creative mind to write in a long-past present tense:

The grass is of a perfect green,
    Dappled with shades this pleasant hour;
The garden-walk is crisp and clean;
    Wind shakes the tears from bough and flower.

Its finest life is in the air,
    Its finest lustre in the light;
And see! The drifting clouds of care
    Are touched with glory in their flight.

(from 'XII')

There is a luminous tuned-in-ness to life here, a commitment to compressing immediate experience into language. This manifests in compounded words such 'Littlemore' and 'Littleless', an indication that Lynch's poetic impulse was at least sensing the possibilities of what Hopkins would later achieve with such force. It is hard to comprehend the critiques of Lynch's work, as he continually fuses his experiences of nature with God – sometimes even to the detriment of the poetry itself. There are only hints that his poetry could be read as libidinous, delicate suggestions that there is some latent sexual yearning related to nature that would trigger conservative nonconformists:

O thou creating fire,
    I feel thy warmth benign;
My hopes a flowering spire
    Arise, unfold, and shine;
And fruits that I desire
    Shall soon be mine and Thine.

    (from 'CIII')

For Lynch, jubilation is an extension of God's love. It shines a spectral light on his writing: 'And if Poetry, as light from the Heart of God, is for our heart, that we might brighten and distinguish individual things ... then must the heart of the Poet in which this true light shineth be as hospice on the mountain pathways of the world'. Lynch was writing against those who only defined God and religion through the negative theology of what should *not* be said. As any poet knows, rules on what can't be said kills creativity in the bud.

A man walks past me in a Puffa jacket, a human fish from the midnight zone, wrapped in ski hat and gloves; Easter was a week ago. He takes a call and mumbles into his phone, 'fair enough, yeh', stepping on a surgical glove, flattened into the earth, dry and crusted, with its fingers tucked inside itself.

Collections of poetry need texture, and *The Rivulet* has that too, hewing its stanzas into different forms, moving between shorter and longer lines. Poem 'VIII' touches on grief, contained within bold pantheistic imagery:

> O, BREAK my heart; but break it as a field
> Is by the plough up-broken for the corn :
> O, break it as the buds, by green leaf sealed,
> Are, to unloose the golden blossom, torn :
> Love would I offer unto love's great Master,
> Set free the odour, break the alabaster.
> (from 'VIII')

There is an acerbic humour at play in Lynch's work too; he later responded to the controversy of *The Rivulet* by writing *Songs Controversial* (1856) under the alias 'Silent Long'. It is in these later poems that Lynch's limitations expose themselves, even as he's flexing his lyric skill. His attack on critics is musical and tight, but then see how the final lines trip over themselves here, as Lynch hems himself in by the end rhymes of his chosen form:

> Crawl, critic, down a ringlet crawl,
>   And maiden virtue teach;
> Crawl, critic, over Samson's locks,
>   His secret strength to reach:
> Crawl on the curly-pated child,
>   And learn his innocence;
> Crawl on the grey-beard, and find out
>   Experience and good sense.
>
>   (from 'The Crawling Critic')

'Find out' and 'experience' cannot scan to the same metrical beat as the rest of the poem. If you're going to attack your critics, make sure your syllabics are tight.

A common ash – branches splayed – forages into the sky; it appears as a broken colosseum in the sky, an empire of possibility, hollowed out from within – now in the final decades of its death. A green parakeet lands on it, whirring like a parody of itself: who's a pretty boy then?

I follow a sharp inner path from the outer boundary of the cemetery, towards Road H. It is just like Abney Park to alphabetize its landscape. Two women are walking behind me, talking about lockdown: 'it feels like a really long day ... by the time you've finished you're tired' ... 'I think the kind of work I was doing ... I was doing alone ... so I'm finding a better balance'. Conversations that once ticked over in pubs sound like prayers here, insides exposed: songs for nature.

What is the legacy of Lynch's work? Miles offered this assessment, one of the last detailed accounts of the poet's work, written over 100 years ago: 'What Wordsworth was in the realm of Poetry in its wider sense, Lynch was in the realm of Hymnody ... Lynch turns from the herbarium of Theology to the fair gardens of Scripture for the inspirations and models of his verse. He is one of the most picturesque of our Hymnists.' Lynch has not completely disappeared from literary culture though and a few of his books are still available today in print on demand editions. Digitisation of this kind synchs with the marketplace – why else would someone produce them? Here is his headstone in front of me now, another path-side burial, passed by hundreds of people every week.

'Popular', Lynch said, 'some poets can never be, and greatest poets never throughout their work'. The will to write may have exacerbated his illness, but without his drive to pick himself up off the floor, dust himself down and hit the next line with wet ink, there would be no trace left of his life at all. His life's work was to resist the long silence that followed.

A hawthorn sits alongside his memorial and a holly tree wraps itself around the stone. Inner rust and outer mould have fermented into a tactile, mottled hue, as if the stone is taking on a lifeform of its own – reptilian – the surface trying to camouflage itself with a new skin. The message is emphatic, a slam rhythm rigging the type to futurity, with just a few individual letters lost from the lines:

TO THE BELOVED MEMORY
OF
THE REVD THOMAS TOKE LYNCH
BORN 5TH JULY 1818
DIED 9TH MAY 1871
[ ]R 22 YEARS MINISTER OF THE CONGREGATIO[ ]
ASSEMBLING AT MORNINGTON CHURCH
HAMPSTEAD ROAD LONDON

A HERALD OF GOD LOVING HIS MESSAGE
A GUARDIAN OF THE LIGHT OF GOD
HOLDING [ ]T FORTH CONSPICUOUSLY
A SHEPHERD WHOSE WISDOM WAS AS
[ ] OLD FOR [ ]HE SAVIOURS SHEEP
AND HIS COMFORTABLE WORDS
A HOSPICE ON [ ]HE RUDE MOUNTAINS
[ ][ ]R [ ]HOSE WHO ARE CROSSING THEM ON THEIR WAY
TO THE PROMISED COUNTRY

Lynch is cast as a herald, a guardian, a shepherd, a saviour; a man offering a hospice, his words a crossing to 'the promised country'. I can't help thinking that this is, in fact, it: Abney Park, the promised country. Birds are singing through the April frost. Right at this moment there is snow in Liverpool and snow on the peaks of Scotland. The past year has brought the kind of crisis that Lynch would have preached his way through by day – and wrote about by night. His last words were: 'Now I am going to live'.

The Garden of Two White Chairs, 1911

Placed back-to-back, like hostages. The Viscountess had positioned them in the centre of the circular lawn; who was she expecting? Of course, she knows enough maritally compromised people to have made this work.

From where I was standing, looking down on the estate, the chairs cast shadows longer than their frames. Flotsam of light danced across the grass.

'DANIEL! DANIELLLL!'

The dreaming ended: time to prepare tea.

'PREPARE THE BEST GLASSES DANIEL, WE HAVE GUESTS!'

I turned my back on the garden but realising I had forgotten the Decanter Cupboard keys, I returned to the room – and there it was, in front of me: the enchanted garden that the lady has talked about so often, the paradise garden I had written off as nothing more than the vapour-trails of her sherry ...

Like a glen, locked in land, it shimmers before me now, coruscating in beatitude, the most beautif

[Document ends. Post-mortem report of Charles Seabright]

Dream Land & Ghost Land

── EDWIN PAXTON HOOD

We know nothing of matters concerning which we know nothing. And so this applies to the ghostly world—always allowing that there is any such world. What do we know?

ARTHUR MACHEN, *THE LONDON ADVENTURE*

'CAN THE EARTH', wrote Edwin Paxton Hood (1820-1885) 'which is but dead and a vision, resist spirits which have reality and are alive?' I am lost in my own book, ready to make another push towards finding a great lost poet. I had my first vaccination this week. AstraZeneca: Astric Forever . A shot of coronavirus genes in the arm, 24 hours of familiar symptoms, followed by the psychic weight of envisioned blood clots. Spend a year thinking the virus will kill you then receive a vaccine which might kill you. Abney's garden gives me the motive for walking it off, for thinking about poetry and eternity – a necessary distraction. Hood was another claimant to the Second Coming, a polymath and a preacher – is he the one I am looking for?

I walk the outer boundary with a description of the

location of Hood's grave, but it's from the 19th century, and the source for this text now eludes me. It gleams on my phone like a religious missive offered to a hidden river:

> His grave is close beside that of Thomas Binney, near the east wall in the Abney House Corner. The memorial may be thus described:-
> A slab of polished red granite covers the surface of the ground. At the upper end of this lies a pied roughly hewn white marble, which serves to elevate the head of a prone Latin Cross of the same material. In the centre of the cross is carved a bunch of lilies, the rest of the space disclosing the words: 'Come Unto Me, I will give you rest'.

Abney House has gone; a modern wall angles into the cemetery, with a row of barbed wire across the top. Beyond it is the fire station, standing on the grounds of Fleetwood House, land that had passed from the Hartopp estate to Charles Fleetwood. Hood's grave – as if pushed forward by the new wall behind – juts onto the path in front of me; a flat slab of salmon granite, brushing against passing shoes. According to the old newspaper account, there were once two or three cypress trees between the grave and the path: 'beside them bloom a few simple flowers'. They are now gone; the path that runs alongside Hood's granite must have been dug at a later date – what use is a garden that can't be walked in?

Victorian lives were often weighted down by over-production; Hood was a 'nonconformist divine', initially preaching on temperance, and officiating in Gloucestershire, Islington, Brighton and Manchester, before returning to Aldersgate in London. There is a weight to the man himself, with the *Gloucester Journal* describing his 'powerful features … the massive, square forehead, the firm mouth, the resolute chin, the penetrating eye.' His personal library was said to weigh twelve tons.

One of Hood's passion projects was raising money for the Royal Hospital for Incurables in Putney. He wrote a pamphlet to raise funds in the year he died, published under the title *The Pamphlet of Pain* (1885). A further subscription was raised after Hood's death, which led to a ward in the hospital being named after him. Hood was also editor of the *Eclectic and Congregational Review* and the *Argonaut*. When asked, towards the end of his life, just how many books he'd written, he said, 'my works number 150 volumes, and nearly all are now out of print'. Hours of labour converted to moth fodder; this is why I am here: to dust off the brittle pages and read them in a new light.

Hood stands out among Abney's dead for his biographies of John Milton, Andrew Marvell and William Wordsworth. He also wrote about two of Abney's interns: Thomas Binney and Isaac Watts. His sermons show a mind drawn to the mysterious, writing about 'The Hidden Life', 'The Power of the Invisible Presence', 'The Creation of Light' and 'Cosmos'. 'Thus all things are doubled in the life of the Christian', he writes, 'he has two lives, he has two deaths'. Hood probes into the unknowable blank of death: 'There is a power by which I am able to live in or with the absent, the distant, and the dead; even in the unknown ... The invisible dead salute us and inspire us in all our selectest hours'.

'Swedenborg removes the veil', Hood wrote in his biography of the visionary philosopher who was so far ahead of the crowd he was able to deliver the news that the Second Coming wouldn't be a physical act but was already taking place through his own writings. Swedenborg's view of the Second Coming as a transformation *through language*, adds to the words written by Abney's poets: 'the Lord has now opened to me the spiritual sense of the Word, and has granted me to be associated with angels and spirits in their world as one of them' (*True Christian Religion*, 776). Hood was passionate about Swedenborg but refused to become an acolyte: 'I am no more a Swedenborgian', he wrote, 'than I am a Bunyanist'. William Blake, too, eventually saw that Swedenborg's cosmos could not contain everything – yet this idea of a Second Coming through language is one that compelled Hood.

There is a movement in the bushes behind me and I

turn; a man with a sweatshirt around his shoulders is walking a Chihuahua, a tormented knuckle of a dog that has been known to single-handedly kill a human. I initially think that the man is talking into his phone, but his love notes are for the dog: 'Not that way silly', he says, maternally, but the dog isn't listening – it is fixated on a distant point, beyond a line of graves.

It is often shocking to find a mind that is so fierce in its ideas and preoccupations – so extraordinary in prose – to then stall in poetry, unable to flex the language to its own singularity of purpose:

> At length I put my brushes by,
> My tinted canvas scarcely dry;
> My hands shall rest until I show
> What pains and labours yet I owe

Hood wrote most of his poems in the 1870s, in the last full decade of his life. The poem above is spoken by a Princess in tribute to an artist she loved, who 'would be / The light of Art in future years'. There is nothing here to catch either the imagination or the ear of the reader; like the canvas described above, the writing is laboured.

Germany provided the impetus for his poetry collection

The Maid of Nuremberg (1873), which despite being written towards the end of his life, exposed Hood's lack of confidence in his poetic talents: 'I do not print this volume from the feeling that there is anything in it really deserving the name of poetry.' The poems are written as dramatic monologues, but without any of the psychological imperative – or compelling language – of Robert Browning. Browning's 'The Pied Piper of Hamelin' appears to be a significant influence on Hood's poetry, which often draws on European folk tales. Hood's gift is in recounting stories, usually from Germany, and foregrounding the weird and uncanny. The *Gloucester Journal* cursorily dismissed his poetry: 'He was a writer of verses of a certain smoothness, some of which, set to popular tunes, are still occasionally heard, but this seems all one can say.'

As I'm thinking about this, a man walks past me in camouflage jacket, face under a hoodie, singing an '80s love song that I have not heard for nearly forty years. Lyrics lost and refound. The cemetery as a depository of stray words; a nonconformist jukebox.

There is a book by Hood that I can't stop returning to, and although it is not a book of poetry, it speaks directly to Abney's transient landscape. *Dream Land and Ghost Land: Visits and Wanderings There in the Nineteenth Century* (1852) aims to bring the invisible to the fore of popular consciousness: 'The opinions of intelligent thinkers in this and in other countries are undergoing a change in reference to the connection of man in this state with the world of spirits … The Discoveries of Modern Science tend to confirm the belief in a spiritual world … Rationalism finds itself altogether at fault in its speculations.' *Dream Land* makes the case for the supernatural, drawing on science for validation – turning rationalism on its head – flouting the sceptics with fact: 'these people have contrived to make what was so settled, quite unsettled; the chambers of mystery have been re-illuminated; and the priests of Knowledge have trimmed the lamps'. Hood argues that the sceptics have led to the opening of the portal: 'he has pushed his enquiries too far; he has opened an unexpected crypt in the vault'. Hood's conviction for the unknown has parallels with Machen's belief in the ineffable mystery hidden under London's surface.

The path bends in front of me, and I enter a section which is dominated by huge memorials. The scale key has been lost in this part of the cemetery: a Celtic cross rises to the size of a bungalow; a huge memorial has been attached to a lump of Paleolithic rock.

Hood would have easily believed that Abney Park Cemetery is a transitory garden. He writes: 'every form of beauty or of terror has its own answering type and correspondence in the next world … it is by spiritual sight that we become familiar with spiritual things'. Like Machen, Hood stands convinced of the power of vision that is innate to all of us and our ability to see beyond the mundane veneer: 'it is in ourself that the power lies to behold,— the vesture of decay hangs round us, but intense vision will ever bring to light the wonderful, and the, till then, unseen'. As with Machen, Hood's conception of the mystery behind the veil is linked to landscape, the ancient path beneath the paving stones, the ghost memory of repeated rituals that remains in the atmosphere of a place.

A woman runs past me, shrieking with excitement, her friend left behind her on the path. The woman's ahead of me now, wearing a blue onesie and a white beret, shouting joyously to the friend she's left behind: 'That's probably the reality, that's probably the reality...'

Dream Land documents the sightings of ghosts seen in previous centuries. The ghost of a woman, dead eight years, witnessed repeatedly in a field in Launceston, Cornwall. An old woman appearing with a pipe, returning to reclaim her property from mis-inheritance. The haunting of the Wesley family house by a ghost called 'Old Jeffrey', murdered in life; doors banging, a shadow in a dressing gown. A headless ghost in Baden, Germany, holding his head under his clothes, saying he must go to the Catholic churchyard at Neckarsteinach ('Germany does appear to be the very Metropolis of Ghosts', Hood writes). The book recounts other strange phenomena. Seers. Telepathists. Doctor Dee's magic mirror. People who can see with their stomach. Hood writes about dreams as a source of the supernatural – the hidden part of us – that becomes visible at night and is alien in daylight.

Hood also wrote a book about Oliver Cromwell, another presence in Abney's dream land. Three years after his death, Cromwell's body was exhumed and taken to Tyburn, where it was hanged and decapitated. There is still some debate over whether this was, in fact, Cromwell's body, but if it was – and many believe this to be the case – there is a possible path from there, to this spot in Abney Park. By the 19th century, a myth had developed that Cromwell's body had been transported from Westminster Abbey, where it had initially been buried, and interred near Watts' Mound. In 1840 George Collison spoke to people who perpetuated this rumour: 'This report I have received from the lips of various old people born in the parish, who affirm, that they have received it from those who were living not so much posterior to the Restoration but that *they* might have had some plausible authority for their assertion'. Collison gives good evidence for the plausibility of this: there are vague accounts of where Cromwell's body was taken for burial, with suggestions it was handed over to family and friends. Charles Fleetwood of Feltwell was one of

Cromwell's generals and owned half of the estate that Abney Park became. He had also married Cromwell's daughter, Bridget. 'It would be a natural disposition of the remains', Collison writes, 'for Fleetwood and his wife to inter them in their own grounds; and the spot to which the tradition refers, would have been at that time, as indeed until very recently it was, the most wild and secluded corner of the estate. It was situated at the extremity of an ancient orchard, and altogether the kind of place to be applied to such as affectionate use.' Cromwell's head has been documented as travelling through London for centuries after his death, a cranial budget box, exchanged for money, its radiant sheen of glazed pork waxing to bone. His remains, however, might be here.

There is a sensuality to Hood's prose, a refusal to see the world through binaries. 'Touch is the key to all the senses', he writes, 'Touch is the principle of all the senses. Perhaps, also, I shall be right, if I say that it is the most subtle of all the senses'. I touch Hood's headstone and recognise a new feeling in me too; I haven't thought of coronavirus since entering the cemetery, and none of today's walkers are wearing facemasks. The emerging spring helps, the slow dispersion of lockdown rules; there is juice in my veins, plans in the diary, and now – from nowhere – a white terrier is sniffing at my feet, and an insect crawling down my back. The year is opening.

Hood wanted to be buried at sea. About a dozen people in the UK do this every year. They are usually from nautical backgrounds, but this doesn't have to be the case. All that's needed is a license from the Marine Management Organisation, costing around £175, and proof that the body is not infected. The corpse is then wrapped into biodegradable clothing. There are even funeral directors who will help with this; Brittania Shipping Company specialises in it. The Thames – or the Mersey, for that matter – are not options; there are only three designated places where this is allowed: Newhaven in East Sussex, The Needles Spoil Ground near the Isle of Wight and Tynemouth. It is possible to propose a new site in your application; coordinates have to be given, as well as evidence to prove it is safe. The dead body is then tagged – in case of drift to the shore – and the coffin needs to be made of softwood with fully biodegradable parts, prepared with holes and 200kg of weight clamped to its base, to ensure that it sinks straight to the seabed. This idea appeals to me, but how much does it cost? Can it be done on a poet's income? I also have a further reservation: a proneness to seasickness. An afterlife of nausea is my vision of hell.

In the same essay – 'Burial Rites and Observances' – Hood wrote of the inner-city churchyards, decrying their state:

There are some spectacles in the world from which one shrinks back with horror, while other circumstances would only create in our minds a feeling of complacent delight. Such a spectacle is the crowded metropolitan churchyard. The feelings which it excites are truly indescribable. The crowded seat of pestilence and death, the torturing memento of the miseries of life, with no whisper of the repose which is beyond: one shrinks from burial in such a town, more than from death itself.

Hood described Père Lachaise as 'the very last place I would wish to be buried in … the dead are not still; it is not a place of peace'. Like many Victorian writers, Dickens included, Hood wrote against the landfill of the city churchyards and was drawn to the idea of the village cemetery. His description still captures a sense of Abney Park as it was and remains: 'some fitful breeze sweeps by, making sad melody, the voices of the dead seem to speak in each hollow gust'.

Hood 'died suddenly in Paris'; his body was wrapped, shipped, and docked near London, where arrangements were made for his burial here. I check the description of the grave from 100 years ago and what I see in front of me defies time: granite unchanged. His memorial is a kind of Cubist artwork, with graphic caps written along each edge:

GREATLY LOVED
AFTER THE DARKNESS TO THE LIGHT

According to the newspaper account, there should also have been 'two clasped hands carved in white marble' with the words 'Within the Veil', written beneath them. I remove a layer of dried earth, and find the hands; then I see the text – a statement of hope in a plague year – with each word separated with a cross:

BE † OF † GOOD † CHEER †

The city's calling me back: the excitement of things to do in real time. A library to reopen. Hours of screen glare. In flesh meetings. Endless to-do lists. Sorry I'm late.

'What is that feeling', Hood writes, 'which causes man instinctively to shudder as he stands on the border of the grave?' In the case of a writer, it is silence. Through his prose writing, Hood walks out of his dream land and ghost land, and into a readership which might still be possible – for his prose at least. He deserves that. With a final clinging to roots and earth, I pull back the side of the grave that is facing the sun, and read:

I † HAVE † OVERCOME † THE † WORLD †

The Garden of the Egyptian Dead, 2950 BC

Abney-Anubis turn me into text in the everafter of my death
For bones without writing are nothing but wretched
Make of my flesh a votive offering
This faulty tablet that is not yet straight on the flanks
Give me power in my feet with lexical secrets
That levitate me to your gardens
There may I never do so much as a day's work
No Teams Skype Zoom Meets
Redact and reprint me forever in your fields

Dreaming a Buried Year

This has been a little digression—I am afraid that there may be one or two more little digressions in the course of this work—designed to show that one should hear and weigh all sorts of messages delivered in all sorts of places. And so I attended with respect and awe to the message that came to me in the tavern in 'the Wood' this spring:

'The leaves are beginning to come out.'

ARTHUR MACHEN, *THE LONDON ADVENTURE*

On 6th February 1892 the *Weston Mercury* reported on the outbreak of a virus which was hitting Stoke Newington with force:

Influenza is still very prevalent in Hackney, Stoke Newington, Islington, and South Hornsey, and it is remarked that doctors and undertakers are busiest men in the district. The latter, in many instances, are working day and night. During last week the staff of grave diggers at Abney-park Cemetery were further increased, and the number of funerals which daily pass along Stoke Newington road is simply enormous when the fact that the cemetery is a private one is considered.

Who remembers now the biggest pandemic of the Victorian

period, the Russian flu of 1889-1894, which killed a million people worldwide? The virus, which probably started in cows, made the Prime Minister ill and caused such mass sickness of workers that it disrupted the transport system. It travelled by rail to large European cities, then to America, and had no known cure – leading to largescale use of strychnine and whiskey as antidotes. Some blamed the outbreak on extra-terrestrial forces; it may have contributed to the end-of-days culture of the 1890s. In May 2020 the Belgian biologist Leen Vijgen suggested that this pandemic induced a range of symptoms that were close to coronavirus; the Russian flu caused central nervous system damage and there were more fatalities among men than women – both of which are common in Covid-19 patients.

Pandemics are a kind of Second Coming. All things wiped, each booking cancelled, stimuli in stasis. I can't stop thinking of Abney's visionaries, those who believed that a huge transformation was imminent. Everything changed. I found my ability for public speaking disappearing because it can't really be called that, can it, looking at a screen in pyjama bottoms while a pile of washing waves at you from the corner of the room? Where were the Archangels in the clouds, the dead rising from the ground – pocked with lead and shreds of ancient newspaper – coming to claim their rightful place amongst the transient millions?

I start to follow dead links. First to Daniel Defoe, who lived on Stoke Newington's Church Street for 20 years, writing *Robinson Crusoe* in the house that still stands. I feel like Robinson, in Patrick Keiller's film *London*, who sets off to find Poe's school and ends up finding Defoe. The writers double each other. Waiting for the lockdown rules to change, I watch the film on loop, vicariously living in a London of the 1990s, which contains a city yet to come. There is something of lockdown in Robinson's tactic of listening to the gateposts in the park as a way of seeing the future: 'Exercises in psychic landscaping, he seemed to be attempting to travel through time'. It is on his walk from London Bridge to Stoke Newington that Robinson has his only moment of hope, passing the Geffrye Museum (now the Museum of the Home) and Ridley Road. I connect with Robinson's view of looking at a place long enough for its past to become visible: 'If he looked at the landscape hard enough, it would reveal to him the molecular basis of historical events'.

Then there's Joseph Conrad who lived at 6 Dynevor Road, a six-minute walk from the cemetery. This was in the years before his books were written, in a hiatus between sea faring, gathering the material for his later novels. Marlow's search for Kurtz takes on all the aspects of a hunt for dead poets. The horror, the horror. Mr Kurtz, he dead.

I make flash appearances on screen for meetings that I never called, talking about endangered poems or experimental fiction – but the connection has gone. The animated gestures of my hands – that my son mocks me for – are no longer in play; shoulders fixed, arms dormant. Sometimes I even forget I'm talking to people, imagine it's an extended talk with the sea, and ad lib or digress for minutes, eventually circling back to the question. This is 'private speaking', a monologue spooled out into broadband via a million Boolean bottles, hoping that the message will reach someone – and that it will mean something. I crave art-spaces – creative conversations – in real time. I live in a brain fog that could swallow London, a peasouper of slow thoughts.

The vividness of my dreams accelerates: one moment I am staring at the same wall, the next I am walking through Hieronymus Bosch's *The Garden of Earthly Delights* as electronic musician Gary Numan circles above me in a plane.

On some days, the ability to conjure a new line of a poetry would be enough to crack my skull in two. A sonnet would be a world to live inside. When the poems come, I live off the internal shock for days, playing the adrenaline like a kite. Prose is a safer bet, ballast to the tides; up at six – before the house wakes – losing myself in the ballerina music of the keys, the rhythm of language. The tap of a vulture, craving the dead. Dreaming the living garden.

The Garden of Earthly Delights, 1491

Gary Numan is flying over the Garden Earthly Delights. Or, as he thinks of it, The God Den of Early Delis. The early bird catches the side salad. He likes that idea, it trips an electronic pulse in his temples, sets off some lost beat that he might just recapture …

Numan looks down from the cockpit at monstrous pink croci, unfurling like labia. Creatures – possibly humans – are moving in its folds. Nymphs couple up on the backs of swine, as a man lures women with a huge fish. Thank you God, Numan thinks, for making me a pilot. A blue globe spins at the centre of the lake.

He is slightly early for his appointment with Hieronymus Bosch. As a luminary – and all music critics agree that Numan is a luminary – he will be the first person ever to detail the exact details of who Bosch was, what he looked like, whether his works are intended as cautionary warnings, or whether they actually celebrate the vices they depict. Big questions. He puts the plane into a holding pattern, by chance over the Land of the Hatchlings – purest nymphs – who have at last broken free of their coronas.

It is then he sees a man, a definite human, walking out from the largest crocus. The man stretches as he looks up at the plane. It is Bosch, Numan thinks, preparing for descent ...

Starry Sky Beneath the Garden

— WALKING WITH IAIN SINCLAIR

My book, then, was to take all these things into account: the old, the shabby, the out-of-the-way; and also the new and the red and the raw. But it was utterly to shun the familiar. For if you think of it, there is a London cognita *and a* London incognita.

ARTHUR MACHEN, *THE LONDON ADVENTURE*

IAIN SINCLAIR MEETS ME AT the Egyptian gates. He's sitting beneath one of the columns, writing something down. We wave and are straight into it, talking about Stoke Newington as literary terrain; Iain is pointing north, towards Ermine Street, the Roman Road out of London. The text on Iain's cap reads: ANCIENT MARINER.

I have asked Iain to walk with me; I want to hear about the Abney Park he knows, the one I first discovered in his work. Given his vast archaeology of forgotten London writers, this might just take me to the dead poet I am looking for, but more than that: here is a great living poet whose poetry exists underground, out of the clinic-light of prize culture. This collision of past and present poetries might just open a rip towards an unseen future.

Non-Londoners see beyond the surface of the metropolis. Sinclair is of both Scottish and Welsh descent, with an artistic line back to Vernon Watkins, and by association, Dylan Thomas. He has also documented the line of doppelgängers which haunt Stoke Newington, writing in *Lights Out for the Territory* (1997): 'I remembered what Poe and Arthur Machen had drawn from this area: confusion, doubled identities, a shift in the electromagnetic field'. I had a plan for the walk, but Iain has a better one: to head to the grave of Edward Calvert (1799-1883) and take things from there. Iain has already been on a recce of the chapel this morning: 'All the things I was talking about are not gone', he says, 'they're just really hard to see, but they're there'.

Iain tells me of Stoke Newington as he first knew it, with the poets Tom Raworth and Anna Mendelssohn both living on Amhurst Road. Mendelssohn was associated with the Angry Brigade's knocking up of low-level bombs and, like Raworth, was writing high-level ones into language. Lee Harwood's last reading was just up the road, 'an elegiac moment', Iain says. These are all major poets who had to make do with fringe activities, the only place that soundbite culture would have them. As a poet, Iain Sinclair is amongst them, consciously writing work that is outside the allotment of the 'pod people', as he describes pre-marketed poets in his *Conductors of Chaos* (1996) anthology. Replicant-writers, cloning poems, appeasing the status quo. Sinclair's strategy for publication has been to release his poems in the smallest editions possible, sometimes as few as ten copies. His poetry resists the folderol of processed poetics, pushing instead towards the unknown: 'the poet strikes out of blind instinct'.

We stop at Mary Hays' headstone, ever-diminishing under the weight of the neighbouring Celtic cross. A woman asks Iain if there is an entrance this way. He directs her with clear and concise steps; to know how to get lost, you first of all need to know the terrain. The more lost Sinclair's poetry becomes, the more collectible. At least by some. As a librarian, I've been backfilling the National Poetry Library collection of his rare editions, a process that the author has contributed to; in 2018 Iain sent one of ten copies of *Fifty Catacomb Saints*, a title that speaks to me of London's lost poets.

Shortly before that moment, a man had turned up at the library one day, an American, saying he was Sinclair's bibliographer. Checked shirt, unshaven, camp bag over the shoulder. Jeff Johnson proved to be so meticulous in his documentation of the author's work that he had even itemised the endorsement Sinclair had given me for my poetry collection *Zeppelins*. Jeff's bibliographies of Sinclair's oeuvre are still appearing, printed in a heavily weighted tan. It had started to feel like one of Sinclair's own fictions: the double taking over the author. Johnson's bibliographic 'Fascicles' are also filled with fragments of lost Sinclair works: omphalos of future prophecies.

Walking towards Calvert, our feet scuffing shale, Iain asks me if I've found a really notable poet yet on my journey into the Magnificent Seven? I update him on Walter Thornbury in Nunhead and Menella Bute Smedley in West Norwood. As I speak, I feel the excitement – and frustration – welling, from living on the verge of a great discovery. Iain Sinclair is the kind of writer you go out walking with and return with a dead poet grabbing at your ankles.

We get caught up in a cavalcade of pugs, a dozen elbows with teeth, jostling on their leads like electrocuted biceps. 'Here's a writer' Iain says, pointing to the bench. The gleaming plaque between us is dedicated to MIKE MARQUSEE, 1953-2015, writer and socialist: 'happiest in Hackney'. In a fitting link with Calvert, Marqusee was a Blakean; unlike Calvert, he did not get to meet Blake himself. Calvert's grave is behind us, marked with hazard tape. A tennis ball appears of its own volition, rolling slowly through the air, like the start of a Kubrick film, but when I look again, the ball is gone. Was never there. A black terrier appears, followed by a middle-aged couple. 'I think', the man says, 'if we carry on going where we're going, we'll get there...'

Sinclair's early poems have the documentary feel of the Kodak, another of his chosen artforms. *Back Garden Poems* (1970) is organised anti-chronologically, from August 1970 to summer 1966; a poetic diary of someone removed, 'with myself / watching other selves'. Aligning with the trajectory of the British Poetry Revival the approach is to perform a thrombectomy on sentiment:

> dead white streets
> as captured
> by a kodak instamatic
>
> (from 'Talking to a Signpost')

It would be a mistake to read Sinclair's documentaries as fact; there is an 'intermesh' of the real and the imagined here, of what he later calls 'true fictions'.

In front of Calvert is a headstone sliced by time, an absence of stone, hovering like a shark bite. Next along is Calvert's. 'Time has obliterated it', Iain says, as we stare at the painter's headstone, which is leaning forwards, face down to its future. I've been given advanced permission to run cold water down the face of Calvert's headstone, in an attempt to bring back the fading words. Magic writing. But the headstone is angled too far forward for the liquid to run down the surface: gravity's pedestal. Iain has an idea, and I fill his cupped hands with water as he throws it on the surface; it darkens the text, but only two words can be read: EDWARD CALVERT.

Iain once walked from Hackney to Hastings, by way of Samuel Palmer's Shoreham and the Golden Valley, a place which had drawn in the Ancients, a small group of artists who had gathered around William Blake in the last years of his life. Before today's walk, Iain had put me on to Raymond Lister's book on Calvert, which gives a rare view of Blake – so often depicted as entranced by visions – also being a telepathist:

> Calvert relates how he saw Blake on this visit, seated at the table in the kitchen ... while the older Palmer sat smoking his churchwarden pipe in the ingle nook, and Calvert sat reading with his back to the candles ... Samuel Palmer had left the cottage about an hour before to go by coach to London. Blake, putting his finger to his head, said, "Palmer is coming; he is walking up the road." "Oh, Mr Blake," one of his companions replied, "he's gone to London; we saw him off on the coach." But Blake was right; and he added after a pause, "He is coming through the wicket – there!" Sure enough, the coach had broken down and Palmer had had to return to the village.

'Calvert himself', Iain says, 'pre-Rimbaud, developed a theory of synaesthesia, sounds would also make colours, and he debated and discussed this with his friends … a pre-Edenic vision, just like one of Calvert's wood engravings'. In the multiplying poplars above us, the birds are at war: trilling attrition.

Sinclair's early poems drew on global poetics, as mapped out by Robert Creeley, Allen Ginsberg and Charles Olson, but also absorb the strange events and trapped energies of the Victorian East End – and the always stranger Stoke Newington. It was out of this gravitational force of London as a meeting space – with the Dialectics of Liberation Congress taking place at the Roundhouse in 1967 – that Sinclair made a film with Allen Ginsberg, which later took published form as *The Kodak Mantra Diaries* (1971).

As we walk, I ask Iain what importance he would attach to the Magnificent Seven in his own mapping of London: 'Very important, really, secretly more important than the sections I've written about, like the M25 motorway, which creates this buzz of low-level conversation around London. Because the cemeteries are much more grounded, they're inspirations, provocations to meditation and contemplation, and the kind of thing we're doing now, the teasing out of lost histories. They are the great stone libraries of the city, all these thousands of erased and disappearing inscriptions and lives, and you tease stories – like in the grave we've seen now – back to Mary Wollstonecraft. It always plays back into the geography. I think the most important thing about the seven, and this one in particular, Abney Park, is that it acted as a destination. If you live in Hackney, where I am now, you are in a place – fixed – but you have these movements, these lines of energy. And the obvious one is to hit on this path of Ermine Street, out of one of the old city gates, and all the way to Lincoln. What flowed into the cemetery was as important as the cemetery itself … the poets I was engaged with belonged to the route of the journey.'

Green parakeets are shrieking over us. A woman passes, with something moving in her wicker basket. 'Then there's Joseph Conrad', Iain says, 'at 6 Dynevor Road, resting from his world wanderings, lodged in Hackney, taking respite at the German Hospital. All of these figures – all of those dreams and inspirations – are flowing up in this direction.' I am starting to think of Sinclair's poems as attempts for gain, to claim ground for what a poem can say, and how it might go about doing it. Sometimes that means occupying negative space – the borders of taboo – sparkling phonemes, the ghost of a flea. To make gain, there needs to be risk.

Iain tells me how he came to Abney Park Cemetery to

make decisions. In his 20s, caught up in an art degree at the Courtauld Institute, it was walking these grounds which brought the realisation that it was time to leave the course and return to landscape gardening.

Sinclair does not write poems for occasions; the poems are the occasions themselves, milked from the grotesque udder of London. 'A city disease', as he writes in *Red Eye*, a book written in 1973 but unpublished until 2013, when it was launched down the road at 110 Stoke Newington High Street. It is a book that absorbs the trapped screams of London's dead – suited and filed – waiting for the resurrection that isn't for them:

> THE DEATH OF ALL THINGS
> BUILDS UP A GRID OF ODOURS
> INTO WHICH WE WALK, WALLS RINGING,
> HUNG WITH INFINITE REGRESSIVE BELLS.

These are the dead I've come to know, metropolitan ghost poets, 'who were dead and able to breathe'.

Iain is ahead of me, camera out, capturing an angel before it falls. Watching him photograph gives an insight into how he writes – quick and with concentration: the full immersion technique.

We walk on, discussing Abney's original arboretum, 'laid out like a library of trees', Iain says, detailing how the trees started at 'A' and worked around by letter. I picture the cemetery as a Ouija board, with me as the planchette – flying manically from letter to letter – spelling out the lives of dead poets. Iain connects Abney's library with the force of its Gothic writers: 'Poe conjured this woodland area as a place where you might meet your own doppelgänger, who haunts you for the rest of your life. Arthur Machen carries on, looking for his paradise in the city, picking Stoke Newington as the starting point for finding this amazing garden'.

I tell Iain about the premise for my book: that Abney Park is Machen's transitory, lost garden. 'For sure', Iain says, riffling through his rucksack for his gummed copy of Machen's *Tales of Horror and the Supernatural*, foxed and annotated, but somehow – like the cemetery – standing up to time. 'It's such a vision', Iain says, reading from Machen's tale:

> For a moment my heart stood still, and I gasped for breath as before me in the place of the familiar structures there was disclosed a panorama of unearthly, of astounding beauty, deep dells, bowered trees, flowers that only dreams can show, such deep purples that seemed to glow like precious stones … well shaded walks that lead

down to green hollows bordered with thyme and here and there the grassy eminence above … architecture of fantastic and unaccustomed beauty.

Looking up from the book, we both intuitively recognise the space we're in for what it is. This is it; we're here in Machen's garden.

Iain was born about four miles from Machen's home in Wales, most of the distance covered by the water of Cardiff Bay. It has been said before that Sinclair does not speak with a Welsh accent but hearing him read Machen's prose – which moves to the rhythms of the Gwent landscape – brings Iain's Welshness to the fore. The words – and the dance of the words.

Lud Heat (1975) is the book in which Sinclair's poetics and excavation of alternative London first converged. Described as 'a book of the dead hamlets', the work connects Nicholas Hawksmoor's eight city churches by drawing lines between them, creating a series of pentagons and triangles, revealing their interdependence: 'white stones laid upon the mud & dust'. *Lud Heat* also shows Sinclair moving the condensed, imagistic detail of his poetry into the prose line. The prose *becomes* the poetry: 'the east London churches still draw the meths-men & derelicts, fire-alcohol devotees, to the attendant parks'. Archaeology as autopsy: the need to see with one's own eyes. The inserted poems in *Lud Heat* are like rips through time, obliterating chronology, gravitating towards the visual. The book is a testament to living on the edge of the occult, being open to the vacuum that can be filled with personal obsessions. In fact, obsession only serves to reveal further truths about the city. Look at things long enough and they start to cohere; the pattern was there all along.

We've found the garden, but where do we find the mythical north-west passage out of London? Iain talks me through the history of this idea, beginning with De Quincey's opium-induced alternative vision to the realities of London – a Borgesian labyrinth of the metropolis – 'this idea that we are caught up in a terrible, enclosed, lost way of confusions and wandering around, and there is, surely, a passageway out of it, if you find that kind of enlightenment or take enough laudanum'. For Iain, Machen's 'N' is a reflection on the idea of finding this north-west passage: 'The other stranger, darker, richer, madder side of it, seems to rely on people like you to dig out the stories. It's very good to use that conceit of the obscurer poets who have ended up here, erased, but they're there, somewhere, and you tease out their stories'.

Iain cites Yeats' quote, about the living assisting the imagination of the dead, which is always a guiding light for me: 'this is literally what our job is', he says, 'to come around here and make some further energy use of incomplete projects and voices that happened to be stilled, with their stone tongues sticking out … I also thought, it was really useful the map you sent me of Abney Park Cemetery, when you look at it, it's very curious…'

I look again (that phrase that is key to Machen's 'N') at the map. I tell Iain that it reminds me of a distended organ, an overworked liver. Iain sees it differently: 'I thought this part of it looked like a chastity belt, with the metal strips across.'

I *look again*: the analogy is beyond doubt, and when seeing it like this, the chapel itself becomes the womb, a geometric lifeform, cradled in green placenta, growing – towards what?

We head towards the grave of Emily Gosse, a figure Iain finds interesting for her manifestation of the tensions between the old ways of Victorian seeing and the 20th-century vision of her son. Iain is ahead, walking the metaphor into reality: 'this is why', he says, 'the area has such a weird sense of ambiguities'.

We stop at the grave of Lancelot Wilde, who 'died at Liverpool'. The condition of this stone is so good – solid granite – it would serve very well for my own, one day. Iain asks if my plans for burial are complete and if there's a spot I have in mind after the years of walking in the shadow of dead poets. How can I answer this question, the one that's been swirling above me like an albatross this year? Surprising myself, the answer spills out, and I say, 'here'. Of course: Abney Park is the landscape of death that renews life; crucible of the stalled resurrection; eternal garden. I ask Iain about his plans: 'Just erasure: cremation. And chuck it in the river. I've got a spot to go in, up the Thames, further up, where it could drift west or be carried back down to London. It's a place we went to when our kids were little; there was a boatyard in Cookham and you could go out there and get a rowing boat and go up the river to find a picnic spot or have a swim. It's gone now. At the end of it you could go to Cookham churchyard.' There is a painting by Stanley Spencer in which the churchyard becomes the site of the Second Coming, the dead clawing themselves up from their graves.

As we walk towards Gosse, Iain talks of the death count in Peru among the Asháninka people – Covid travelling up the Amazon from Brazil, the huge number of deaths, the impact on the rainforest. 'There's no environmentally friendly way of dying', Iain says, 'apart from composting.' The most environmentally sound burials will be in the future when human composting has advanced. This involves putting the corpse into a tower, built on the same principle as a garden compost. The body is laid flat, with sawdust and woodchip underneath, and takes about six weeks to break down, eventually becoming food for plants and shrubs. It does, however, leave the same problem as a box of KFC: what to do with the bones afterwards. It is estimated that this saves about a ton of carbon over cremation and traditional burial. I think about the emotional aspect of this: grandma as a bag of compost, ready to be scooped into the roots of a shrub, visions of her winking from a leaf. I like this a lot – for its simplicity and for the giving of the body back to the earth that sustained it – but it misses one thing: the headstone. The page in the stone library.

I realise I've overshot along the path to Gosse, and we turn back, finding the Little Elm Walk which has grown beyond recognition since I was last here. 'If you see hazard tape', I tell Iain, 'let me know'. A wall of cow parsley faces us; we wade in, looking for the tapered slate of the Gosse headstone, one step at a time – potholes and broken stones covered with bindweed. I reach for a huge obelisk, stabilise myself on its skinny pyramid, and then spot Gosse a few metres away, covered with summer vines. We approach and Iain reads the text: "The dust' – I like that – 'the dust of Emily Gosse". Iain tells me that he walked past the Gosse house yesterday, on Mortimer Road, with its plaque that records only the husband Phillip and son Edmund – but does not mention Emily. Next day he is here, ringside to the poet. He continues with the headstone recital: "waits here the morning of the first resurrection' ... When's the second one? Is it like first class?' These are the questions that every Victorian wrestled with. Iain sneezes; the dust lives on.

I turn and Iain is gone. I spot him down at the base of a neighbouring obelisk – the one I leaned on before – text-sniffer, reading out the words on the memorial for C.W. Hunt, a music hall lyricist. It is interesting to see Iain's preferred method of working in action, moving forward through impulse and intuition.

We find our way back to the path. 'If we nip in here', I say, 'we might get a couple of poets'. I am trying to get us to the grave of Isabella and George Banks, but this part of the cemetery is so overgrown now. All has changed beyond recognition since the early Spring. We return to the path, leaving the husband and wife curled in the recovery position. Then comes another massacred headstone and a hip tomb which is open at the side. We check inside for poets: nothing. Only an alphabet of litter and broken sticks. 'It raises the question', I say to Iain, 'who is a headstone ever for?' 'They're a series of prompts', he says, 'for people like you to come along and write about them'.

Walking towards the chapel, Abney's crucible of strangeness, we talk about Arthur Machen. 'I'm sure Machen would have walked around here', Iain says. 'He liked the pubs in Stoke Newington. This cemetery would have hit his double interest: the theatre and his fascination with death and resurrection.

He was a Catholic so he would have been uneasy. You know the book *Authors Take Sides on the Spanish Civil War*? They were all Republican; only two supported Franco. One was Evelyn Waugh the other was Machen. He saw it as a religious war'. This is familiar territory; be wary of your literary heroes when it comes to politics. Nettles in the daisies.

We arrive at the chapel for the first time today. Iain points out the X at the centre of the window's Celtic cross. He wrote about this in *Lights Out for the Territory*. X marks the spot. Then he points at the outer wall of the chapel, where the outline of a Satan figure is visible, faintly daubed into the bricks. Only later, when I check my photographs, do I see that there are two Satans. One short of an Unholy Trinity. Iain's ahead again, skirting the outside hut. He points inside: the site of the GOD GOES WIRELESS graffiti. Detritus and the fag ash of winter fires.

On the verge of the chapel, I show Iain the grave of Reverend Hibbert Newton and talk him through the dead poet's intensities: British Israelism, Millenarianism, anti-popery. Iain spots something in the headstone: the shape of a figure, emerging on the surface. Arms outstretched, a skull shape writing itself through bacteria. Self-publication.

We arrive at the colossus of the Watts' statue. Iain reads: 'The joy we labour of their tongues'. It fits with his reading of

Abney's chastity belt system, a kind of spiritual foreplay. We talk about Watts' work in laying out the grounds that became Abney Park Cemetery, the visual poem that we're caught inside now. An adjacent memorial has a rusted barrier around it, a series of spiked wheels, attached to a metal bar. A Ben-Hur's chariot of memorials: death slicing the ankles of unwieldy cyclists.

The book that has been on my mind to ask Iain about is his most unknown: *Fifty Catacomb Saints*. He has described it as his 'invisible book'. This work is Sinclair's sustained act of literary ventriloquism, a voice-throwing carnival in which the dead are gifted back their voices, their imaginations assisting the living. Sinclair's prose is poetic, but these are prose poems, the form that Rimbaud used for space travel.

Catacomb saints – or Katakombenheilige – were disinterred burials from 16th century Rome, which were then sold to shrines and religious houses in Germany as 'a mastercard opportunity'. In their new homes, they were given 'invented biographies', and put on display as a way of drawing visitors. Sinclair extends this concept to speak for the zeitgeist of fraud, sleaze and corruption; the duplicity of the Catholic church becomes synonymous with the corporate greasing of our cities.

As we stand surrounded by London's own catacomb saints, Iain talks about the background to his strange, compelling poems: 'they started to sculpt new creatures out of these bones, totally randomly, and the nuns made incredibly elaborate outfits, with jewels etc, and they became shrines in all these German churches. They were just total inventions. Then they would write biographies of these saints, that had never existed, so you have this fictionalising approach to bones … You can scramble language in the same way and create new structures out of bits and pieces. The poems come out of a number of journeys, to Palermo, a little bit of Mexico, and a series of walks, including Van Gogh's, whose walking in England was epic. So I began to trace his walks. He walked from Ramsgate to London, then from London to Welwyn … I fed in bits and pieces from other stuff, to create a kind of mulched, collagey, free-flowing, semi-prose, semi-whatever, work … it felt like a freedom to do it in that way, grabbing in things from what I was reading, becoming part of the same structure.' The result is a dense, spectral weave, that speaks as much for the death-in-life of corporate greed as it does for London's living dead:

The second catacomb saint is buried in a tall window, heraldic arms spread wide, as if holding a damp sheet. In an outsourced collegiate dining room overlooking the ancient cathedral city, the saint bows before soup. Part-tenured, our man has an unfranked passport to the martyr's shrine. In this country, they murder blood as a formal requirement. You do your hand too much wrong. We levitate, sir, and perish like sparrows.

How can work this good remain unnoticed, slipped under the creased vellum of the culture, waiting for its readers? 'I didn't want to inflict it on anyone', Iain says, 'so I just did ten copies. Most of the writing I was doing was for commission, with somebody looking over your shoulder. This felt like what I would do in the Albion Village Press days, when it didn't matter, as no one would read it, so I just did ten copies. It was going back to the origin in a way.'

Fifty Catacomb Saints garners energy from the torsion of past lives pulsating against the backdrop of political corruption and capitalist megalomania. 'The main impetus', Iain says, 'was taking the lid off and letting rip, assembling creatures and journeys from fragmented memories, echoing quotations, dictation from the dead and aborted pilgrimages'. And within this intoxication of the text, Abney Park itself appears, site of so much of Sinclair's work, shimmering city of new life and decomposition:

I come by this lengthening road to Abney Park, in such glorious weather, as before, decisions to make, the biggest deferred, to join the company or step back from the neurosis of composition. I was never the sixteenth saint ... A felled angel lies at peace among bee-mimicking hoverflies and a pillow of fire-damaged ash.

Abney: the magnet drawing the filings to its centre.

I ask Iain the question that's been on my mind: whether he publishes these small editions as a gesture towards being a lost, living poet? 'It's not so much a positioning of myself', he says, 'as a recognition of where that kind of writing can go now, which is sort of nowhere. When I started, we were doing a hundred copies, which was what the market of that moment could stand, because there were another hundred poets themselves who kept in touch with what you were doing ... then I felt the market shrinking and there can't be more than about ten people now who would be interested in reading this. I'm happy to do this, in order to write the kind of work I really want to write'.

We head towards the grave of Edwin Paxton Hood, the chronicler of invisibility. We find the red granite of his grave and Iain looks down on it: a conjuror of his own dream land and ghost land. We talk about the Victorian tension between science and mysticism, the invention of strange machines that could conjure up visions of the afterlife. Behind us is the haunted island of the dead Cedar of Lebanon. Iain has a hunch that if we decided to wade into the undergrowth, at any point, we would find a dozen more poets.

We land on the fringes of Conder, buried increasingly deep in the entanglement. The sun is flogging down on my neck, birds trilling: summer has found us, crooked over the graves. Conder with his one eye, switching on the ears: the synaesthesia of dead poets. I tell Iain how Conder travelled the entire world without leaving his desk in north-east London. Apocalypse in a drawing room. 'It would take some lifting to get this off', Ian says, looking at the hip tomb. A school visit passes behind us, children chattering, excited, discovering again that the world is networked.

Standing at Conder's grave, I read some of his words: odd transitions, grasping at an epic vision, guided by angels towards eternal portals. Iain recalls the Welsh preachers of his childhood, nonconformists who could sermonise themselves into reverie, occasionally stumbling into poetry. Congregations become captive audiences. The blurring of text into hymn. 'At the end of the 19th century, you might have got the sense that this was the moment: a turn of a century, after London has changed so much, dramatically from the 1840s, with the railways and the canals opening up. Suddenly it explodes.'

We decode the shaking hands that is prevalent on so many headstones here: freemasonry and the slipping between worlds. Ian reads out a text: THE PRIVATE GRAVE OF CHRISTIAN FELDMAN. What kind of grave isn't private?

Thomas Robertson – Dramatic Author – appears: the grandson of nobody. Then the blown-up Blue Peter badges of William Booth, founder of the Salvation Army. We hover with the mayflies on the pathway leading to Alexander Japp. We walk along the path of broken headstones to the proscenium arch of the fallen tree. A further series of hazard tape markings have been left for me; the pathway towards the incandescent Scot is clearly marked. 'It looks like some kind of police incident', Iain says. I mention to Iain that Japp was a friend of Robert Louis Stevenson. 'Gosse was too', he says. London's dead poets usually gather around Dickens: bluebottles rimming the treacle. In Stoke Newington, Stevenson becomes the luminary, a guide in this land of doubling. 'I've found and lost Japp twice', I tell Iain.

We follow in, under the fallen tree, and I realise now why Japp is hard to find. I can see his grave, low-lying under a hood of trees, but to access it we need to circle back on ourselves through a miniature, compressed forest. Fallen memorials form steps.

'Down here?' Ian asks.

'I'm not sure we'll get through?'

'I think we will,' Iain says, and he is walking ahead, peeling back the branches, stepping over a fallen tree. This is how writing is made: watch out for nettle stings. We find Japp, for the third time, and Iain reads the memorial: 'Death is but birth in other realms more rare'.

We make our way back towards the chapel, past an angel with a missing head and a missing wing. Iain tells me how the chapel was always the centre for local amateur occultists, who came to enact various rituals. William Lyttle, the 'Mole Man' of Hackney, whose description by Iain in *Hackney, That Rose-Red Empire* (2009) must have led me to have a dream of a man digging beneath the streets of London, creating his own subterranean garden landscape. I tell Iain about the pig's head, found in 2009, an extension of the weirdness that Iain discovered when he first arrived here in the 1960s: 'It felt pretty dark, you were wary of coming around here at certain times of day. It now feels very benign, almost like Hampstead Heath'. Abney Park is in its post-exorcism era. The dark rips in time might be closing, but time always loops back on itself, and it is possible that this lockdown garden could transform into a bleak landscape at any moment.

As we walk, I find myself saying, 'Let the chapel draw us in to it', and it does. We have circled back to its inexplicable geometry, where Zach is waiting to give us access. A clank of iron oxidized by rain. Ripped netting, rippled with pigeon shit. The sun cut into Celtic currency by the window. Our voices change here: acoustics weighted by time. Soon the chapel will be transformed, regenerated, sealed and heated – a venue for weddings. I realise then what gives the chapel its dominance: the bodies lying around it, the unfinished energy of their life stories, their extant work. The bodies of dead poets trying to rise through blocked funnels. 'Abney Park outflow', Sinclair writes in *Lights Out for the Territory*. 'Broken texts washed free from their headstones. Erased letters forming a new language'.

§

A few weeks later, Iain sends me three new poems. The tendrils of the cemetery's grounds reach out into London, where the poets are making a comeback.

COMMON ASH; *or,* STARRY SKY BENEATH THE GARDEN

'...*when* he hath tried me, I shall come forth as gold.'
   --- Job. XX.111.10

Tap roots of the burying ground move south, encroaching on the City, soliciting custom, and offering, as trees must, chemical transmissions. Worthy human hosts are prepared for planting. Older angels, *remiges* clipped, feathers of primary flight damaged, are always attended and supported by new growths. It is constant, this traffic. Poets and preachers and children. In communality of absence. The founding Brook waters hungry shoots in a cultivated wilderness, pierced by a network of suggestive paths. Climbing blindfolded towards the light.

ARRIVAL

'Hackney money laundering,' she joked, 'involved me washing the small silver coins picked up on a morning's walk.'

Hostage to truth, the reforgotten poet lies
weighted by an inkwell lighthouse in schist.
He's caged in softly whistling ribs.
Slate tongue stamped with fictions.
It's not his story to tell.
This was never London, in truth, but
another paradise garden, name forgotten.

EMILY GOSSE

O perfect circle without commencement
kick now at dappled fieldstone
release the other Emily, headstrong agoraphobic spinster,
always in transit, wheels hidden beneath her weighted skirt,
between choking rooms of tedium, crying bliss,
she has wrestled still wet, unresting
incestuous sheets, slate slippage, and *made*
the proud bolster stand --- Omphalos! --- Ermine Street ---
chthonic surge, couplings behind the arras,
revenge! Verse fitted only for tract, meanly modest--- flame!
In anticipation of horrid ointments, she stays, 3 hours in silent
converse before spitting grate, shamelessly flushed.
Lichen script will map faster than a borough architect.
Fossils of things that were never born. Elective pain!
Talk if you must of seaside pleasures, 'fair Greek and good Hebrew'.
Fathers and sons, unwifed, redeem their time, by conjuring
proliferating networks of white thread, ghostpipes.
A single solitary teaspoon of soil is better than an ocean of disbelief.
Attractive odours of the provisionally deceased. Intelligent fungus
has no corporeal form, shape-shifting without stain,
but something out there is struggling to tip the marker stone, drowning
in cow parsley, until you agree to spend and spend --- or speak

§

The Garden of Molemen, 1996

Have you ever entered a garden from underground?

There are ways of knowing what is above. Roots, to start with. Whole entangled fists of rhizomes, wound and entangled into dried hearts. A fistula gorging on nutrients: dried ears listening for clues from the other side.

These are the signs of the growth above. But what else is there? This depends on the nature of your topsoil; if it is too clay-like, it prevents the moisture from seeping down below and the roots can't penetrate the surface.

Molemen like me have tried every type. The surfaces I exist under come in every consistency. What you think of as your floor is my roof. Your rejectamenta – my epiphany. Your rainfall – my hydration.

Strangest things I've found? A rosary. An American dollar. An idol. Nobody can say how long these things have been here, except the dollar of course. And the rosary. Actually, probably the idol too

– if you know about that kind of thing. I wrap a plastic bangle around each object, date it, treat each one like a foundling. They become part of my museum.

I have met other molemen who tell me that the underground itself is their museum, that by removing the artefacts from their natural element I am destroying their energy. But I am an explorer and I need to return with my findings. To leave empty-handed would be like a space mission without the footage.

Of course, there are constant complaints about my work. Those who say the earth will collapse, those who fear for their house. Terraces sucked into landfill. All the urban myths.

Occasionally, I misjudge distance, and my hand comes pressing up into a garden – a sandworm expanding into air. If I end up in yours, reach out and shake it.

Just leave the idol where it is.

The Art of Sinking

—— DR ISAAC WATTS

I cannot help dwelling on the manner in which I associate these early literary discoveries of mine with the places where they were made.
ARTHUR MACHEN, *FAR OFF THINGS*

'I AM A VILE POLLUTED LUMP OF EARTH', states Isaac Watts (1674-1748) in his first ever poem, written when he was seven years old; a self-attacking acrostic, with the first letter of each line spelling his own name vertically down the page. So begins a life of endurance – and a life in language.

The poem is in the book in front of me now, as I stand on Watts' Mound, a secluded lump of mud in the north-east corner of the cemetery. Watts loved the view over Hackney Brook in the days before it was culverted into London's sewers. In the early days of the cemetery, the path to the Mound was wide open; these days it follows a narrow, hidden route, past the grave of a John Whitaker Nutter. It is easy to miss the turning.

Watts spent the last 16 years of his life in the now demolished Fleetwood House on Stoke Newington High Street.

He was a chronic doodler, pencilling on the walls some 'emblems of grief and death, mingled with the arms of Gunston and Abney, and intended doubtless to honour their memory' (Quoted in Reverend John Stoughton's *Shades and Echoes of Old London*, re-quoted in Bridget Penney's 'The Hunter'). This is the kind of ghost-written, hidden tract that brought Machen to this corner of London.

The Mound has changed since Watts knew it. Not only has the view of the brook and the heronry disappeared; so has the chestnut tree, which was planted at the centre of the Mound. There is another tree here now, a sweet chestnut, but it is not the one that George Collison describes as being covered with the 'vulgar and inexcusable ... initials of numerous visitors ... cut in its bark'. The ancient orchard has gone. Collison describes this as being removed 'to allow the boundary wall to be built, and because the trees, overgrown and crowding upon each other, required to be thinned'. There is another tree here, locally named Pinus Mysterious because it has eluded all attempts at classification. It is one of several uncategorisable pines in Abney Park, a throwback perhaps to the arboretum: cross-pollination in the intractable garden.

Watts is a unique proposition in the Magnificent Seven. He is a poet who not only lived within the landscape I am walking in, but also wrote his poems in the grounds themselves. And more than this, he actually played a part in the design of the original arboretum that would later become the cemetery. He is mooted to have planted a row of elms that now form the Little Elm Walk. But there is a problem: Watts is not actually buried here – he could not be, as he died before the cemetery opened – and is instead interred in Bunhill Fields, in the same land as William Blake.

Richard Gee has described Watts as 'Abney Park's resident patron saint' and like all saints, his presence here is a part of the miasma. When Watts was sixteen, he successfully applied to the Dissenting Academy of Stoke Newington; following his education, he lived as a private tutor with the Hartopp family at Fleetwood House. When he began to experience a recurring illness, he was invited by Sir Thomas Abney to live in his home. Watts spent the rest of his life with this family, most of it in Abney House. Watts is still here: in the Mound, the statue, the Walk named after him. There are few poets whose presence manifests in a place as much as Watts does in Abney Park. This was a life in retreat from the metropolis, in the village of Stoke Newington, before it simmered with the slow-burn of an inner-city borough.

Watts wouldn't have known it at the time, but when he helped Lady Mary to design the grounds of Abney Park, he was laying down the parameters of a landscape that would eventually hold around 200,000 burials. As Paul Joyce argues, if it wasn't for Watts' writing, we would know much less about the history of this unique terrain.

There is something else remarkable about Watts. He is the only poet I have encountered in my walks through the Magnificent Seven who could be said to have influenced William Blake. I like to picture Blake as a boy, crouched over a book – an intense knot of red hair and flesh – with his poetic sensibility beginning to whirr, compelled by the musicality and precise forms of Watts' poems. As Mona Wilson writes in her *Life of William Blake*:

> It has been suggested that Blake in composing the *Songs of Innocence* may have acted on the hint in Dr. Watts's preface to his *Divine and Moral Songs for Children*, which he describes as "a slight specimen, such as I could wish some happy and condescending genius would undertake for the use of children and perform much better." There is no doubt that Blake had read the words of Watts.

A quick comparison between Watts' 'Song 3, The Rose' and Blake's 'The Sick Rose' shows that this is undoubtedly the case; the contrast also shows how far Blake wanted to take Watts' ideas into a new realm, writing poems that troubled the moral certainty of the earlier poet:

How fair is the Rose! What a beautiful flower!
    The glory of April and May:
But the leaves are beginning to fade in an hour,
    And they whither and die in a day.

    (Isaac Watts)

O Rose thou art sick.
The invisible worm,
That flies in the night
In the howling storm:

Has found out thy bed
Of crimson joy:
And his dark secret love
Does thy life destroy.

    (William Blake)

Watts had written his moral songs to instruct children away from 'idle, wanton or profane songs, which … become the seeds of future vices'. Adult hypocrisy dominates Blake's poems, many of which are written from the perspective of children rather than being aimed *at* them. Watts is estimated to have sold seven million copies of his book, published across six hundred editions. In his own lifetime, Blake sold less than 30 copies of his. Blake's poetry was reviewed in the *Monthly Review* in 1806 as 'certainly very inferior to Dr Watts'. I stand on a sawn log stump, to try to get a view of outside London: portacabins and terraced housing. An ancient ash hovers over the Mound, left to decline, providing wood mould for the cemetery's natural ecosystem. I recall how Watts had also influenced Emily Gosse; one of her tracts tells the story of a girl who has been led to Jesus through a providential encounter with one of Isaac Watts' hymns. Across time, Abney's poets speak to each other.

The Mound is like a stage; a heavy slab of solid mud banked with huge stones. Creeping ivy grows around its edges. I take a deep breath and stare in the direction that Watts would have looked: a moss-lined wall and above that, the old and new builds of Stamford Hill. I circle the Mound, making a flawed attempt as an estate agent, assessing it for opportunity: a one-room bungalow on a historic site. Easy access to Stoke Newington station. Basement space. One previous occupant (Cromwell).

Watts is barely known as a poet; his legacy lies in the 750 or so hymns he wrote, which began a mass movement of hymn writing across the Christian world. Hymns such as 'Our God, Our Help in Ages Past' and 'When I Survey the Wondrous Cross' rework the text of the Psalms of David into metrical and stanzaic form and influenced later hymn writers such as John Wesley. They continue to be sung by thousands of people around the world today. As biographer Graham Beynon writes, 'His title as "the father of hymnody" comes not because he was the first, but because he went further and wrote better than those before him'.

A sparrow flies past me, with a caterpillar dangling from its beak. A green parakeet leaps from a scaffold: birdman pretending to be a bird. Then comes another blackcap, with its strong, reedy song; its head dipped in ink: mail-stamp. Birds are following me. Last night I dreamt that I was watching the raven from Poe's poem scavenging amongst detritus; and as I watched I realised that the bird was already in its perfect garden.

In *Hymns and Spiritual Songs* (1707) Watts saw his hymns and poems – or 'spiritual songs' as he called them – as akin to each other, simply using section dividers to split them. How does Watts the poet stand up today? One of the most dynamic and trusted literary establishments of today, the Poetry Foundation in Chicago, has published a long essay on its website, crediting Watts as an 'important minor poet'. Watts has undoubted gifts as a poet, but he rarely allowed his art to be anything more than an extension of his pastoral work. *Hymns and Spiritual Songs* includes a list of contents at the back of the book, which allows readers to find his poems by topic, for example, on 'care of the young and feeble'. For Watts, his art was always inextricably linked to religious mission, which raises the question: can great poetry be written with the aim of providing a specific moral purpose to its readers? Watts was aware of the line he was straddling here: 'I have endeavoured to please and profit the politer part of mankind, without offending the plainer sort of Christians, so in this it has been my labour to promote the pious entertainment of souls truly serious, even of the meanest capacity, and at the same time (if possible) not to give disgust to persons of richer sense and nicer education'. It reads like a brief from a marketeer, angling a new product that aims to break down segmentation amongst audiences; Watts wants to reach both the 'mean' and the 'nice'. A poet, I think, should always try to surprise themselves in the act of writing and – occasionally – be unsure what they have written, relying on their own intuition of its own literary worth. This is how unique styles develop. For the most part, Watts' poems are a series of dispatches, written to extend his missionary work.

Drilling starts in the bushes next to me: workers are renovating the cemetery wall. Their signage reads:

UNIVERSAL STONE
DANGER
CONSTRUCTION
WORK IN PROGRESS

The workers break into fits of laughter as obstinate crucifixes stare at them like line managers.

Watts lifted many of his chosen poetic forms off the shelf, and had no interest in devising new ones:

> The metaphors are generally sunk to the level of vulgar capacities …
> If the verse appears so gentle and flowing as to incur the censure of feebleness, I may honestly affirm that sometimes it cost me labour to make it so: some of the beauties of poetry are neglected, and sometimes wilfully defaced; I have thrown out the lines that were too sonorous and have given an allay to the verse, lest a more exalted turn of thought or language should darken or disturb the devotion of weakest souls.

Here is a poet who does the unthinkable: wilfully strips back their most musical lines for fear the reader will become distracted. The technique of deliberately 'lowering' language to accommodate less educated people was known at the time as the 'art of sinking' and Watts speaks openly of this aim in his poetry, wanting to 'sink every line to the level of a whole congregation'. He wrote as a preacher first.

Watts' main contribution to poetry as an artform is his book *Horæ Lyricæ* (1706), subtitled: 'Poems chiefly of the Lyric Kind'. It is divided into three books: I. To Devotion and Piety; II. To Virtue, Honour, and Friendship; III. To the Memory of the Dead. Not surprisingly, I am drawn to the third section, looking for poetry as tombeau: elegies for the deceased.

The thought starts me thinking about Cromwell again; I stamp mud from my boots. Is it possible that I'm standing directly above the bodily remains of the Lord Protector? A quick decision needed to be made on Cromwell's burial; there was family in Stoke Newington, a carriage, spade – quiet corner – no more said. My money is on a spot just off the Mound, where the ground dips into a curved wall. The man from the Fens cramped into a London bedsit. Grumbling isotopes. Give Me Ireland.

Most of Watts' poems are not in the tradition of the personal lyric but are instead clearly argued descriptions of God's power. When Watts distinguished his poetry from 'all the Heathen poets', he was also separating himself from the ancient Greeks and Romans such as Sappho and Catullus (although he does draw directly on Pindar), as well as the blood and sex of the Jacobeans. It is in holy writing, Watts argued, that 'God is creating the world'.

Watts was less interested with the world inside, as the one that is already created *for* him – and he comes nowhere near the rapture of Gerard Manley Hopkins. If Watts were alive today, he would have used his poetry to argue that coronavirus was created by an angry God:

> The mischiefs that infest the earth,
> When the hot dog stars fires the realms on high,
> Drought and diseases, and cruel dearth,
> Are but the flashes of a wrathful eye
> From the incens'd Divinity.
>
> (from 'Divine Judgements')

Aside from the unfortunate construction of 'hot dog' here – another example of language mangled by a changing world – Watts would never criticise God for vengeance of this kind; fault is always to be found with humanity:

> What are my eyes but aids to see
> The glories of the Deity
> Inscrib'd with beams of light
> On flow'rs and stars? Lord, I behold
> The shining azure, green and gold;

But when I try to read thy name, a dimness veils my sight.

(from 'Self-Consecration')

There is no swerving away from the influence of John Milton on Watts' poetry. The focus on sight – and light – as linked to faith are established Miltonian constructs. Watts takes this forward in his work by fusing short and long lines together, creating a music of counterpoint. He might have taken this even further, but his reservations about *Paradise Lost* attack many of the poem's strongest aspects: 'The length of his periods, and sometimes of his parentheses, runs me out of breath: Some of his numbers seem too harsh and uneasy. I could never believe that roughness and obscurity added anything to the true grandeur of a poem'.

I stand on a brick and realise I can see into someone's back garden: a private rosarium, roses stamping their vermilion into sandbrick. Transitory fistulas. I lean against the pin oak that has been planted at the centre of the Mound, its branches splayed in all directions – reaching for the light. Next to it is a statue of a woman in robes: beige, muddied and headless. The statue's head has been replaced with a lump of pitted stone: swamp mutant, swimming against the tide of Hackney Brook. Lost muse; its head a bulb of corona.

The past year of lockdown has brought too much mind and too little body. Standing here on this mound brings a different perspective; this is a spot for poetry readings. It has been an odd time for living poets, who are used to the regular fizz of packed spaces, the human connection of live performance. This is one of the few spots from which you can't see the chapel; for a long time it was the highest point in this part of London. The view is blocked with hawthorn leaves, which always bring Blake to mind, my walks on Peckham Rye – documented in *Cenotaph South* – the dialogue with angels. Once you've seen Abney's chapel you cannot unsee it: lightning rod to the clouds. Transmitter of text. God conductor.

Watts was in constant dialogue with the dead; it was his job. His poems in 'The Memory of the Dead' include elegies for King William III; for the sudden death of a Mary Peacock; and a poem 'On the Death of an Aged and Honoured Relative'. 'When I recollect the victory of my friends that are dead', Watts writes, 'I frequently rove in the world of spirits, and search them out there'. Watts also writes for the people he lived with on Abney's land, including Thomas Gunston (brother of Lady Mary Abney). It is here we have some of Watts's clearest writing about what would become the grounds of Abney Park Cemetery:

How did he lay the deep Foundations strong
Marking the bounds, and the rear Walls along
Solid and lasting; there a numerous train
Of happy Gunstons might in pleasure reign,
While nations perish, and long ages run,
Nations unborn, and ages unbegun:
Not Time itself should waste the blest estate...

Ye dusky woods and echoing hills around,
Repeat my cries with a perpetual sound:
Be all ye flow'ry vales, with thorns o'ergrown,
Assist my sorrows, and declare your own;
Alas! Your Lord is dead.

Woods, hills, vales: the foundations of the current cemetery. Meadowland extended northwards for miles; a palatial eight miles of shrubbery now dreamt into municipal space. The never-ending orchard.

I lower myself to the ground, to hear – or perhaps just sense – the invisible Hackney Brook. Could I have a water cremation? Also known as Resomation, the body takes about six hours to dissolve, with the use of lye and heat. The method goes back to 1888, when Amos Herbert Hobson developed a method for processing animal carcasses into plant food. The body is placed in a pressure vessel with water and potassium hydroxide, and heated to 320°F. The home of all my sensory pleasures reduced to a green-brown soup, the bones soft as Chinese mushrooms, dissolving to ash in the hand. It's not as environmentally harmless as it sounds; it takes hundreds of gallons of water to create this human Pot Noodle, although some environmentalists champion it, due to it using about a quarter of the energy as a cremation. Ashes to ashes, mush to mush.

Watts is at his peak when writing about pain. He suffered ill health for most of his life, writing a group of poems entitled 'Thoughts and Meditations in a Long Sickness, 1712 and 1713'. This is his most interesting work, drawing us in to the collapse of his body and the inability to compartmentalise 'reason' from physicality. The Enlightenment duality between body and mind begins to creak; a worldview compressed in Watts' skull – the binary clamp. Watts spits squibs of ink, his writing providing shelter in the storm of breakdown. He is held back by the duality of his thinking, but this was a failure of the time he lived in; Watts separates his 'nervous disorder' from the mental torment. The unstable foundations of this worldview begin to creak and Watts writes his best work – a poem that is linguistically alert and dynamic:

When little restless atoms rise and reign
Tryrants in sovereign uproar, and impose
Ideas on the mind; confused ideas
Of non-existents and impossibles,
Who can describe them? Fragments of old dreams,
Borrow'd from midnight, torn from fairy fields
And fairy skies, and regions of the dead,
Abrupt, ill-sorted.

Here is the ore in Watts' output, a confessional poem that draws us into the eye of the storm of his personal crisis, momentarily removing God, making the reader a confidant to this moment of despair. As a result, there is far more happening in the middle of each poetic line, as Watts bypasses the stricture of end-rhyme, moving his work towards Milton's blank verse and sewing together images with natural flair:

If I but close my eyes, strange images
In thousand forms and thousand colours rise,
Stars, rainbows, moons, green dragons, bears, and ghosts,
An endless medley rush upon the stage,
And dance and riot wild in Reason's court
Above control.

Watts' sequence thrives on the compression of scale, expanding out towards God and the cosmos, then shrinking back into the veins and arteries of his body:

> Hast thou not seen
> Each restless atom that with vexing influence
> Works through the mass of man? Each noxious juice,
> Each ferment that infects the vital humours,
> That heaves the veins with huge disquietude,
> And spreads the tumults wide?

(from 'Peace of Conscience, and Prayer for Health')

Watts runs this close to dissent, for if God can't say what happens inside the body, then the matter must be left solely to scientists. In Watts' world, the ramifications of these thought are radical; good health can be orchestrated by the scalpel and not only by God's divine judgement. There are moments that recall Marlowe's *Doctor Faustus*, with Watts marvelling at the majesty of 'the spheres', reminding himself that he must believe in God as the overseer. It is here that Watts forgets about 'the art of sinking' and uses his poetic skill as the forceps to retrieve live matter from personal crisis, explaining that, 'Long afflictions are soul-searching providences, and reveal the secrets of the heart and omissions of duty that were unobserved in a day of peace'. Suffering gives insight, and here he edges close to the 'dangerous sonnets' that he warns his readers to be wary of.

Two dogs turn the bend of the path to the Mound, and head straight for me. I stand still, cornered. They sniff my leg – no bones, just books – and run back in unison, weaving in and out of each other. Over the wall behind me, I notice a security camera is perched like a love bird, inexplicably aimed into the cemetery. Ghostwatching.

Watts wrote about eternity and the Second Coming in *The World to Come* (1745), written when he was in the final years of life: 'Who can take a survey of the resurrection of the millions of the dead, and of the tribunal of Christ, whence men and angels must receive their doom, without the most painful solicitude, "What will my sentence be?"' There is no carpe diem in Watts: every hour on earth is an hour longer to prepare for death. 'Death is the king of terrors', he wrote, envisioning the dead rising in rank and file, as Christ sits on the jury. Watts died without a fear of death, with an assistant writing down his words: 'It is a great mercy to me that I have no manner or fear or dread of death. I could, if God please, lay my head back and die without terror this afternoon or night … I have no fear of dying; it would be my greatest comfort to lie down and sleep and wake no more.'

Isaac Watts died on 25th November 1748, aged 74. The epitaph on his headstone in Bunhill Fields downplays his contribution; a Puritan blade, slicing through the immense body of work that he left behind: 'after fifty years of feeble labours in the gospel, interrupted by four years of tiresome sickness, was at last dismissed to his rest.'

§

A few weeks later I'm back in the grounds, making a video with Zach. The plan is to read Watts' poem about the Second Coming, 'The Day of Judgement', against the backdrop of his monument. It is the end of an afternoon of tangled ends along the Boundary Path; poets that just won't rise, cruisers spotted amidst green parakeets, the living garden, knotty with life. Later, I watch the video back, my voice hoarse from hours of speaking through a facemask. 'When the fierce north wind', I begin – in sunlight – as an elderly woman lingers at the railings behind me. Her friend points up at the statue – have Watts' lips begun to move? A terrier's bark slices through the birdsong. 'Such shall the noise be, and the wild disorder'. Zach zooms out from my reading, slowly revealing Watts, and an ancient elm, gnarly and entwined with dead branches: a mast of thorns. 'See the graves open', I read, 'and the bones arising'. A man walks past, caught on camera, his face a steamed bun between a flat cap and scarf. The news that the buried garden is blooming is yet to reach everyone's ears. 'While the living worm lies gnawing within them'. A jogger flies past in blue, arched back, looking upwards. The weather is changing, clouds darkening:

> When the fierce north wind with his airy forces
> Rears up the Baltic to a foaming fury,
> And the red lightning with a storm of hail comes
> > Rushing amain down, [...]

> Such shall the noise be and the wild disorder,
> (If things eternal may be like these earthly)
> Such the dire terror, when the great Archangel
> > Shakes the creation

A child runs towards me, her mother behind. A man walks languorously; no aim, no agenda, his backpack slacking down the back of his legs.

Then a raindrop lands on the page before me, staining the word 'creation'.

The Garden of the Lost Raven, 1845

N.

The lost raven steps out from the poem.

NE.

Meat-loving raven : freed from the text.

NEV.

Starved raven : wrought ghost of dying embers.

NEVE.

Raven in its reeds : boneyard in vellum.

NEVER.

The wet bead of a jet-black shutter : raven's eye on Insta.

NEVERM.

A Corona crown on raven's head : latter-day saint of bin day.

NEVERMO.

Raven with a post-it on its back : 'Unhappy Master of Unmerciful Disaster'.

NEVERMOR.

Slammed on old stout : raven makes a jukebox from a yoghurt pot.

NEVERMORE.

Promoted : bouncer at the lair of the white worm. Not your scene tonight mate.

NEVERMORE!

Tropic Death

—— ON THE SEARCH FOR ERIC WALROND

Genius, art are, I take it, vision; the power of seeing further, seeing deeper, seeing more than we others see.

ARTHUR MACHEN, *THE LONDON ADVENTURE*

LOCKDOWN BREAKS. On 25th May 2020, a 46-year-old black man called George Floyd was arrested in Minneapolis for attempting to buy cigarettes with a counterfeit $20 bill. By 9.25pm that evening he would be pronounced dead. Floyd had lost his job at a restaurant due to the coronavirus.

I'm thinking about this as I walk away from Watts' Mound, dodging puddles. Rain overnight. The paths have returned to gruel-shaped pools, quickly drying in the sun.

All year time has been out of flow, a consequence of grief, as Denise Riley writes. This murder of a black man is not uncommon in itself – especially in America – but this has happened at a moment when the need for human compassion is at its peak; a moment when there are no distractions from the horror. I see the effect of Floyd's death on my colleagues of colour;

some disappear from screen culture, or move cities, to be reunited with family.

Abney's landscape has often offered refuge to the black community of Stoke Newington. The 2011 census showed that 17% of residents of Stoke Newington were black. In her novel *Mr Loverman*, Bernardine Evaristo configures the cemetery as a place that draws the Antiguan-born character Barrington:

> Late at night, whenever I got the urge, I used to tell Carmel I was taking my evening constitutional, or goin' down the pub, or whatever, when in fact I was making excursions into Abney Park Cemetery. It was like wild countryside back then, with brambles, trees and hedges that provided camouflage for all kinds of covert negotiations.

Then I had the kind of conversation that happens once, if you are lucky, in the lifecycle of writing a book. I was at the Visitor Centre and Haydn says, 'And of course, we have Eric Walrond buried here'. This is a new name to me, and she hands me a copy of *Tropic Death* (1926), the only book that Walrond published in his lifetime. These ten stories contain some of the most atmospheric writing on landscape I have read, alternating between the Panama Canal region and Barbados – with another story set in British

Guiana and another on a ship between Honduras and Jamaica. The prose simmers in the linguistic virtuosity of dialect, the tropical heat of places that couldn't be further removed from Stoke Newington:

> The western sky of Barbadoes was ablaze. A mixture of fire and gold, it burned, and burned – into one vast sulphurous mass. It burned the houses, the trees, the windowpanes. The burnt glass did amazing color somersaults – turned brown and gold and lavender and red. It poured a burning liquid over the gap. It coloured the water in the ponds a fierce dull yellowish gold. It flung the corn and the peas and the star apples a lavender glow. It pitched its golden, flaming, iridescent shadow upon the lush of paw-paw and sunflower. It withered the petals of rose or sweet pea or violet or morning glory. Its flame upon the earth was mighty. Sunset over the gap paralyzed. Sunset shot weird amber tints in the eyes of the black peons ... sent strange poetic dreams through the crinkly heads of mule boys tiredly bowed over the reins of some starved-out buckra cart horse.

Startling metaphors, personification, assonance, alliteration, anaphora – the list of poetic techniques gives the density of a prose poem. This is prose, like so much poetry, that demands to be read out loud. As Walrond's biographer James Davis argues, '[it] is as much about its sound as its sense, that sound is its sense'. And more than this, we have Walrond's unique vision as a writer, his commitment to presenting his characters as aspects of their landscape, as organisms grown from their socio-economic reality. Walrond is fascinated by places, the details of what makes them unique, and how they impact on people. Beauty becomes 'paralyzed', the sun becomes 'weird', and – most importantly for me – the impact of it all is to create 'poetic dreams'.

Abney, too, is a landscape of 'poetic dreams'. I collect names as I walk towards Walrond's grave: Ebenezer Spencer, Matilda Farmer Friday, William "Willie" Chrees. As in George Saunder's *Lincoln in the Bardo*, it is easy to imagine the dead talking together here after dark. *Tropic Death* is quite literally a book of the dead; every story involves someone dying.

Vast amounts of information about Walrond's life have been synthesised in James Davis's remarkable biography, *Eric Walrond: A Life in the Harlem Renaissance and the Transatlantic Caribbean* (2015). As Davis points out, *Tropic Death* 'is populated by ghosts, spells, and the return of various forms of the repressed'. Three of the ten stories involve characters succumbing to supernatural phenomena. Walrond was a huge fan of Poe, and the American Gothic is here reclaimed through Carribbean folklore and Anansi tales, drawing heavily on the high mortality rate of West Indian men working in Panama.

A whip-thin man in khaki walks past me, his head balanced in the scales of his headphones; he is carrying a tiny espresso, balanced between his fingers like an idol. It must be the late-night YouTube jukeboxes with Sarah. Last night I had a dream that I received a spam email that pulled me into the video of Talk Talk's 'Life's What You Make It', watching as Mark Hollis pounded out a rhythm on a piano and animals moved in the bushes around him. I then read the text of the email which told me that Mark Hollis had got lost in a garden and learned something so terrible that he retreated from the public eye forever.

Stunned by the discovery of Walrond I read *Tropic Death* in days, with the unequivocal satisfaction of encountering a work of genius. How, then, has Walrond become so forgotten as a writer? Can I claim him as a poet? And how, I wonder, did he end up buried here in Abney Park Cemetery?

Walrond was born in British Guiana in 1898 to a father native to that region and a mother from Barbados. Walrond's father left them when Eric was eight, at which point Walrond moved with his mother to Barbados, before returning to the Americas to live in Panama, at a time when the famous canal was being constructed. Panama became Walrond's spiritual home, as he would later write: 'I owe the sincerest kind of allegiance to it'. Panama seems to have hugely excited Walrond as a site of linguistic diversity and cultural exchange. It also created tensions between people, and these personal and interpersonal struggles would be absorbed into his later writing.

Walrond's mother brought Walrond up within the Plymouth Brethren, which connects him with Emily Gosse; she is buried in a direct line north from Walrond's resting place on Watts' Walk. Despite Walrond's love for Panama, this was also where he first encountered racial prejudice, writing: 'In Panama, where thousands of British West Indians had settled, I got my first taste of prejudice – prejudice on the grounds of my British nationality! The natives were a ... race of Latins with a strong feeling of antipathy towards British Negroes. But their hatred of us, curiously enough, had been engendered by our love of England'. It was out of these tensions that Walrond's career as a journalist began; this was continued in New York, where he arrived on the cusp of the Harlem Renaissance.

Walrond landed in New York in June 1918, working variously as 'salesman — porter — dish slinger — secretary — elevator operator — editor — longshoreman — stenographer — switchboard operator — janitor — advertising solicitor — houseman — free lance'. Racism jolted his efforts to become a journalist, writing in an article called 'On Being Black':

America is a big place; I feel it is only a question of time and perseverance. Encouraged, I go into the tall office buildings of Lower Broadway. I try every one of them. Not a firm is missed. I walk in and offer my services. I am black, foreign-looking, and a curio. My name is taken. I shall be sent for, certainly, in case of need. "Oh, don't mention it, sir.... Glad you came in.... Good morning." I am smiled out. I never hear from them again.

'I am smiled out': the ultimate microaggression. Walrond visits an optician who suggests he adopts the style of glasses that black chauffeurs go for. Walrond feels the urge to say: 'Don't think every Negro you see is a chauffeur'. He offers his services to various newspapers, experiencing either outrage or silence. Walrond's adopted position, perhaps to save his mental health, is to feign naivety, as if wondering why there should be any problem with him asking for work to begin with.

What would have been flagrantly obvious to black Americans, particularly those travelling north to escape Jim Crow laws, could be downplayed by a West Indian immigrant, experiencing the city for the first time. I wonder how much of this experience played into Walrond's depression, which he would later describe as his 'old shifting, restless, nervous moods'. He would write in a letter written around this time: 'There is really a self, a side of me, I think, that is not bad, not undesirable, but as fate would have it, this side has been for some time submerged by the harsh rulings of life'. By 1925 his depression was so bad that he would write to Joseph Freeman, 'I am actually engaged in the absorbing process of counting the minutes of my existence—as if I were a condemned man'.

I think of my own depressions, the first that lasted years, the second crackling with anxiety. I heard from an old friend recently, who told me about breaking down last summer, seeking treatment and medication. One of the many free of the virus but hit hard by Covid-19. Somehow – this time – so far – I have avoided a further depression. The runs to the beach have helped; Abney's garden has bailed me. Perhaps there is some degree of good fortune in this too and over the past week, Walrond's prose has sent my synapses firing. How have I lived this long without it?

Walrond eventually broke through as a journalist with *Negro World*, a journal edited by Marcus Garvey, the Jamaican political activist and founder of the UNIA-ACL (Universal Negro Improvement Association and African Communities League). Walrond became assistant editor of the journal after winning its literary competition for a story which depicted Garvey as 'the prince of men'. In addition to these prose pieces, I discover something deeply exciting: Walrond is also said to be the author of prose poems. After weeks of feeling myself becoming more immersed in a genuinely luminescent writer – Abney's lost genius – I take a pause for breath: is Walrond the lost poet I've been looking for all these years? Do his prose poems – written with the intentionality of being *read* as poems – stand up to the brilliance of *Tropic Death*?

'A Black Virgin'

For a long time I sit there dreaming—dreaming—dreaming. Of what? Of the fortunes of the flower of youth? Of the curse of bringing a girl of her color into the world? Of fight, of agitation, of propaganda? No. Clearly separating my art from my propaganda, I sit and prop my chin on my palm and wish I were an artist. On my canvas I'd etch the lines of her fleeting figure. […] Her voice. I wonder what it is like? I go to her. "Will—will—you please tell me where I can find a copy of "Who's Who in America?" I startle her. Like a hounded hare she glances at me. Shy, self-conscious, I think of my unshaven neck and my baggy trouser knees. I fumble at the buckles of my portfolio. Those eyes! I never saw anything so intensely mythical. […] "Why yes, I think there is one over there." Her voice falls on my ear as the ripple of a running stream. Her face I love—her voice I adore. It is so young, so burdened with life and feeling. I follow the swish-swish of her skirt. I get the book and she is gone—gone out of my life!

My first reaction is to dispute that these are prose poems at all; they are closer to flash fictions. They are often narrated from the perspective of a roving poet character and draw heavily on the kind of symbolism Poe employed in his tales. Walrond was clearly feeling the pull of poetry that was around in 1922, but his desire to tell a story dominates over the enclosed language world of poetry. It was a time of great fluidity between literary genres; and these 'prose poems' are actually far less poetic than the stories in *Tropic Death*. They are too concerned with *telling* things, opting for flowery, cliched expressions, such as 'intensely mythical' and 'the ripple of a running stream'.

It is interesting to compare Walrond's pieces with other poetry published in *Negro World*, which was largely lineated and formulaic. Looking at the limits of the poems that Zora Neale Hurston contributed to the journal would give no indication of what she would later achieve in prose. As a journal that made no claims to be advancing literature, *Negro World* allowed writers to experiment with poetry, perhaps usefully allowing them to make mistakes. Walrond was writing his way towards the storytelling of his later work and these hybrid texts perhaps helped him to formulate the kind of fiction he wanted to produce. He didn't have long to wait; the ascent towards his mature writing happened incredibly quickly, taking just a few years. Just as the character in this story senses an internal shift from politics to art, the same would happen to Walrond; tensions with Garvey led to Walrond leaving *Negro World* in 1923.

I can't deny my disappointment that Walrond's 'poems' are not the lost manna I am looking for, but the feeling doesn't last for long; Walrond was only in his early 20s when he wrote these pieces, just a few years away from writing *Tropic Death*. After *Negro World*, Walrond signed up as a cook's helper on a ship, heading to the Caribbean. It was an experience that would help shape at least one of the stories in *Tropic Death*. Then there was a galvanising moment for the Harlem Renaissance Writers; a dinner at the Civic Club in 1924, in which Walrond and other writers met with New York's influential publishers. This led to an anthology, *The New Negro* (1925), which included one of Walrond's stories. Walrond's work was also promoted by Edna Underwood, a literary agent, who circulated his work further, leading to publication in the *New York Herald Tribune* and *Vanity Fair*. He would also publish in Charles Johnson's *Opportunity*, which has been described as the 'root' of the movement; Walrond eventually became its business manager.

Walrond was also dynamic in circulating his work himself, something which became easier as he developed a reputation. Ethel Ray Nance later wrote: 'He would go out and seek editors and publishers, show them his work … He had a newsman's sense of timing.' He attended Regina Anderson's literary salons; David Levering Lewis commended him about 'his accented, rippling wit, his urbanity and fearless independence'. Walrond was thriving, opportunities counterbalancing depression; he was at the height of his personal and literary confidence, a man who stood out in a room of people. Nance wrote:

> He was very pleasant, but as soon as he entered a room, you knew he was there. He moved very quickly, he couldn't stay still in one place, especially if he was excited, and he was excited most of the time. Either he had met someone or else he had a new idea about something and he would have to walk up and down when he described it or when he talked to you. He had quite a way of meeting strangers, anyone who ever met him remembered him.

It is an odd thought, remembering strangers. I wonder how many of the people I have walked past today I will actually remember? Perhaps these two approaching me now, a woman who looks like Lizzie Siddal, strayed from a Pre-Raphaelite painting – crimped copper hair – and the man she's with, wearing a Futurist silver jacket, like Hugo Ball at the Cabaret Voltaire. 'I've literally just seen Katie', he says. 'What, now?' she asks. There is an urgency to the exchange: live matter amidst an audience of the dead.

Walrond wasn't just propelled by a movement or on its fringes; he was a central force, creating opportunity for others. Through him, the zeitgeist went further. And as quickly as he had become a central figure in the movement, Walrond left it behind, just as his book became one of the most read titles at the 135th Street Library. He won a Harmon Award and received a Guggenheim Fellowship (one of three black recipients out of 75) to write an ambitious non-fiction book called *The Big Ditch*, a history of the Panama Canal. He left New York to undertake some initial research, but he also rushed at the book at a time when his publisher was beginning to experience financial difficulties. Furthermore, there was a stipulation from the Guggenheim that his grant did not allow him to write the book in the United States. Walrond would never finish the project, and only fractions of it would appear – over 25 years later – in the journal for the asylum he was admitted to in rural Wiltshire. A vast ocean away from his years and success in Harlem and a step closer to this plot in Abney Park.

A sparrow flits from a bush and lands on the path before me. It stutters like a drunk on an A-road; pauses, processes, retreats. Then a branch falls from a poplar, playing the snare on the way down. A cloud cancels the sun – London has a million weathers.

Walrond found his way to England via Paris, where he lived near Montparnasse: the peak of the poets. *The Paris Tribune* wrote:

> Eric Walrond, another Guggenheim scholar, is living with Countee Cullen. He is hard at work on his next novel, which we hope will be as interesting as *Tropic Death*, published a couple of years ago. Walrond ... has travelled extensively but considers the Left Bank the bright spot of the cultural world. "Its traditions and literary associations," he says, "stimulate the best efforts in one. Here one can find variety or peace."

Walrond drank at the Dôme, a favourite haunt of Henry Miller and Hemingway, and enjoyed the nightlife. In 1930 he moved to the French Riviera, and became friends with Nancy Cunard, whom he had first met in Paris. Walrond's depression followed him, along with an anxiety over the terms of the Guggenheim Fellowship, and his inability to finish *The Big Ditch*, which was beginning to live up to its title. This was exacerbated when Boni & Liveright dropped the book altogether. Embarrassed by breaking the terms of the Guggenheim and increasingly low spirited, Walrond arrived in England in 1931 and rented a room near the Crystal Palace: a Modernist in view of the Victorian birdcage. He wrote as a correspondent for the *Baltimore Afro-American*, which carried a short, biographical account of his life here, embellished and romanticised:

> Eric Walrond, one of the better writers, has made London his temporary hunting ground. He has the energy of a dynamo; gets up at seven in the morning; drinks a cup of tea in bed, reads the daily papers, smokes at least five cigarettes and then settles down to work. Writes until noon and then for a hike in Hyde Park, back to his desk at two thirty and writes until six. Drinks gin and chews spearmint gum while typing. Claims that England is Virgin territory for young colored men and women of letters; intends to stop here until the field is properly explored.

In London, some of Walrond's stories were accepted for the *Spectator* and the *Evening Standard*. Walrond quickly became attuned to the country's history of colonialism and what he described as the 'colour bar', which prevented opportunities for black citizens, inevitably leading to economic deprivation. Walrond aligned with Marxists in the city and began to write about colonialism from the angle of capitalism. He wrote of African slaves, 'His lot was no better than oxen and sheep—with which he ranked in the white man's scale of property values'. Walrond moved to a flat near Tottenham Court Road but struggled to find a publisher for his fiction. It is an old story: the struggling writer in London, kicking dust in the backroads, looking for a key to the city. In Walrond's case, this was a reality exacerbated by racism: doors closed, not today, thanks.

I arrive on Watts' Walk – a narrow path, lush with nature on either side. Walrond is buried somewhere here, in this thoroughway of the buried garden.

In 1938 Walrond was involved in a workplace incident in which he stabbed a co-worker. Although he was charged with 'maliciously inflicting grievous harm', he was acquitted. Walrond's adversary had claimed that Walrond had invented rumours about him, and when he approached Walrond about it, they got into a fight. Walrond had pulled out a small penknife, which he carried for cutting newspaper clippings. He slashed his colleague on the arm and, as they struggled, Walrond stabbed him again. At the court case it became clear that the man had been a wrestler and a nightclub bouncer; he was the main adversary of the fight, which Walrond had responded to in self-defence. The judge was discerning enough to see this, though this stressful situation must have affected Walrond's mind and mood even more.

Walrond was living near the British Museum when news of the Second World War was announced; before the bombing began, he joined a mass exodus from the city. He took a train to Bradford-on-Avon, where he lived as the only black resident in a town of 4,000 people. With Harlem – and the cafés of Paris – still pulsing in his memory, he stayed for 12 years, living just a few miles from Stonehenge.

So many burials are packed in closely to the edge of the path here; cracks in the stone lead to graves. As I walk, head down, names swim into view: A. E. Pearce, Sgt Major; Olive Peveril Wilson; Elizabeth Godfrey; Rose Cook. Tendrils weave between the words.

In a bizarre twist, there is a possibility that Walrond was an RAF pilot during the war; in April 1944 the *Chicago Defender* reported that Walrond had disappeared in an airstrike over Germany. Walrond also wrote an article for the *Amsterdam News* with the byline 'Somewhere in England':

> In an old Flemish weaver's cottage, I sit and listen to the starlings and the grunts of pigs far down the terraced slope. The hum of aircraft is incessant. Sometimes they fly low or circle round and round before zooming off again. Above the green tops in the valley, smoke is issuing from the chimney of the town's one factory. Before the rearmament of Britain began, the factory was engaged in the production of tennis balls. Now, on a day and night shift, it is turning out munitions.

I pass the War Memorial, which has been adopted as a picnic area. Last time I was here, a man took a leak on some nearby headstones, then leaped the wall onto the memorial perching, with his legs dangling, to eat a box of fried chicken. THEIR NAME LIVETH FOR EVERMORE, the monument reads.

After the war, Walrond worked in a rubber factory; in 1952 his depression became so bad that he admitted himself to Roundway Psychiatric Hospital. He took his unpublished stories with him – and his pages from *The Big Ditch*. His experience with the Harlem Renaissance soon manifested, and he galvanised the inpatients, making things happen, soon becoming the Assistant Editor of the *Roundway Review*, the hospital's literary journal. The bright young thing of the Harlem Renaissance – the one who had given so many people hope for the future of black writing – found himself writing for an audience of mentally ill inpatients in a sleepy corner of rural Wiltshire.

In 1957 he left the hospital and returned to London. It is a testament to his commitment to poetry that the last project he worked on was the *Black and Unknown Bards* event, which took place at the Royal Court Theatre in 1958. Walrond was invited by Erica Marx of the Hand and Flower Press to gather poems for the event. This led him back to the British Library and into meetings with influential people such as William Emrys Williams, Head of the Arts Council, and the editor of Penguin who had been responsible for setting up Pelican Books. They discussed the possibility of a major new anthology of black poets, for which Walrond would write a 10,000 word introduction. This was a new phase in London, a decade after HMT Empire Windrush had arrived at Tilbury Docks; the contribution of Caribbean people to British culture demanded visibility. Walrond moved to a room near Bedford Place, but was soon downgraded to student accommodation in Bloomsbury; he was so poor he could not afford a typewriter. He moved north to the cheaper district of Hornsey, in north London, just three miles from this spot in Abney Park. By this point he had become a background presence in the planning of the *Unknown Bards* event, though Hand and Flower Press did bring out a small anthology of the work that Walrond had gathered. It was a project that he said took far more time than the 43-page pamphlet suggested.

I look back to the chapel and consider the permanence of its rose-like windows, which were designed to fit with the arboretum. Stone flowers, sculpted by hand. A butterfly lands in front of me, on the path-side, and slowly closes the pages of its wings.

James Davis describes Walrond's last occupation as working for export firms based near St Paul's. There is an account of him bumping into a Jamaican friend in a nightclub. 'He had very special hours', the friend said, 'he'd go in and have a drink'.

I have brought my copy of *Tropic Death* with me; there is no writer who can invoke place like Walrond. His prose crackles with the energy and peculiarities of the Tropics. His story 'The White Snake' speaks back to this place, with its different fecundity of earth – and somewhere nearby – the culverted Hackney Brook.

> Coral earth paved the one flake of road in Waakenam. Gathering depth and moss, the water in the gutters beside it was a metallic black. It was a perfumed dawn—the strong odor of fruit and turpentine flavoring it. For it was high up on the Guiana coast, and the wind blew music on the river. Vivid flame it blew on the lips of grape and melon, and ripened, like the lust of a heated love, the udders of spiced mangoes and pears peeping through the luscious grove.

There are no mangoes or pears here, in Walrond's part of the cemetery, but it is a luscious grove. An ash tree is growing behind his headstone; its trunk has become a platform for climbing ivy. Mystic power, strength, spirituality, endurance – the tree symbolises so much of Walrond's life. This is a knotty, gnarly landscape, a rising bank of tangled matter. The chest tomb of a Mary Clayton is layered with moss, like the baize on a snooker table. Death racks them up.

Tropic Death revels in syntactic distillation, like so much of Modernism; just as *Ulysses* can easily be seen as a work of poetry, as well as being a novel, the same case could be made for Walrond's stories. Most descriptions of the book detail its poetic nature, with the blurb stating: 'There is poetry, folk essence in it'. Wallace Thurman wrote of Walrond: 'None is more ambitious than he, none more possessed of keener observation, poetic insight or intelligence'. Like Joyce's work, Walrond's stories ask us to read them on their own terms, to forget the parameters of what we think a 'story' or 'poem' should be. The book was published shortly after Jean Toomer finished *Cane*, another major Harlem Renaissance work which was written in a mix of poetry and prose. I was disappointed to find that his early pieces – the work claimed as prose poetry – does not have the brilliance of *Tropic Death*, but I will gladly accept poetic prose of this quality into the sphere of my series. I say it then: I have found, at last, a buried genius in the Magnificent Seven. Not a great lost poet but an exceptional writer of poetic prose. His marginalised place in literature requires a radical re-centering – right back to this exact spot I am standing on.

Opportunity in poetry is uneven; I set off to prove this in 2014, when writing *In the Catacombs*, and Walrond is the strongest evidence I've found since. His genius for atmospheric language creates works that cannot be found anywhere else, but colliding factors worked against his flow as a writer: his inability to meet the terms of a Guggenheim fellowship; his publisher dropping *The Big Ditch*; his itinerant years; poverty; racial oppression; depression. He was faced with the resistance of London to black writers, even those who had thrived in the early phase of the Harlem Renaissance. A world war stifled his progress further, a global crisis which took a further six years from his writing life. One moment he was dancing in Paris, the next trapped in an asylum.

The bank rises behind Walrond's grave; there is technically no way of knowing where he is buried. This is a spot for unmarked graves and he could be buried on either side of the path. The headstone was only placed here in the past 20 years; for decades after Walrond's death, there was no indication that he was buried here at all. In its way, this is a landscape of deep verdure; an intermingling of Japanese knotweed, holly, nettles, wood avens and dock leaves. A sapling gingko tree is growing to the left of Walrond's headstone. An occasional leaf – early summer casualty – abandons its branch: man overboard.

Walrond wrote: 'My work and my raison d'être are to depict my race's existence, its history, its suffering, its aspirations, and its rebellions. There is a rich source of emotion and pain there. It is there that I draw the elements of my work, and it is in the service of the black race that I devote my activity as a writer.'

I've read about a silver birch that was once struck by lightning here on Watts' Walk; it survived with a gash down its trunk. Watts already has a statue and a Mound in the cemetery. It is time, I think, for a renaming of this path: Walrond Walk.

After several heart attacks, Walrond collapsed on a London street in 1966, shortly after hearing that Liveright – the publisher who had dropped him 30 years before – wanted to reprint *Tropic Death*. Walrond was encouraged by this, and – ever the perfectionist – made some amendments to the book. He was dead on arrival at Bart's. News filtered back to America, with Arna Bontemps writing to Langston Hughes: 'Have you heard that Eric Walrond died in England a couple of weeks ago? It was a heart attack (about his 5th) on a street in London.'

Walrond once wrote of himself: 'I have had … to punch myself and say: '*I must be dreaming. This surely is not you, Eric.*' Eric, the black boy from a race once in slavery!'

The sun is beating a path through a crosshatch of branches and the fizzing sap rises. There is no headstone like Walrond's here; it is an elegant, Modernist tablet, white against the landscape's green, and includes an ideogram of four symbols set in relief on the stone – sun, path, feather and book. It has the condensed visual symbolism of Walrond's work. The image of the sun and the path seem to align into the figure of a man, who is writing in a book with a quill. Someone has planted a greater periwinkle next to the headstone and I snap it on Picture This: 'Your plant's leaves are yellowing due to a lack of fertiliser', the app tells me.

So I take out my copy of *Tropic Death*, and read it out loud.

The Garden of Diminishing Fame [SPAM], 2021

Have you ever considered, in your most intimate and lonely moments, perhaps at night, when the house whispers with the cobwebs of past regret, just how it might feel to completely disappear forever and leave nothing behind? For a small subscription we can now help you to achieve this plan. Due to never-before-seen evidence from the life of Talk Talk frontman, Mark Hollis, we can reveal how the secret of such a disappearance was recorded in the video to that hit song everyone knows: 'Life's What You Make It'. Within ten years of writing this, Hollis would achieve that mythical reality and disappear from the frosty glare of public view.

The video of course takes place in that most strange and enchanting of London gardens: Wimbledon Common. The footage unrolls, revealing the Common we never see, the one at night, where a badger's rear disappears into a hedge, and the face of an owl appears – like a moon in itself – and the wily fox scurries. Then come the smaller critters of urban gardens: the scurrying spider, a centipede winding its way forward on its many legs, and an army of woodlice, equipped for small accidents of misfortune with their shields on their back. All the while, Hollis plays at his piano, seemingly protected by his sunglasses, the cold night evident on the icy breath that comes from his mouth as he sings, and a roving light circles in the trees above.

But this you already know. What we can now reveal is how Hollis becomes cognisant of a force beyond the veil of this nocturnal landscape, and was so struck that night by unspeakable horror, that he would retreat from public life, never to make an appearance for the last two decades of his life. The answer to this mystery is in the circular floodlight that can be seen, in close detail, for much of the video. Notice how the moths circle its white, dazzling pan of light. It was here that Hollis saw the shapes that the moths formed as they danced against the light, creating a temporary message scripted by their wings, revealing a message of such insidious evil that no human mind could bear its dark truth, leading the artist to inevitably succumb to the after-effects of its revelation. What was this message? For a limited reduced plan subscription this can be revealed to you now, just click below to read for yourself what Hollis saw with his own eyes, on that fateful night.

The Second Coming

After that night ... I went home and thought it all over. There seemed no more to be done. Still, I felt as if I would like to have another look at this singular park, and I went up there one dark afternoon. And then and there I came upon the young man who had lost his way, and had lost—as he said—the one who lived in the white house on the hill. And I am not going to tell you about her, or her house, or her enchanted gardens. But I am sure that the young man was lost also—and for ever.

ARTHUR MACHEN, 'N'

'Gather us in', the bones of the dead say, 'and lift us high'. The second life is coming.

This is how I want to be buried: dressed in a Fall T-shirt and a velvet jacket, in a biodegradable coffin, the box doused with red wine as it is lowered into the earth. If Abney Park Cemetery is accepting internees by then – or wishes to make an allowance for a haunter of its grounds – take me there. To be part of this stone library, not too far from Eric Walrond, would be a fitting end to my project. Zach recently sent me a photograph of a grave he found: Florence and John Joseph McCabe, interred by 1944. Who knows, they might be family?

Or bury me in my heartland, Liverpool. Anfield Cemetery would suit me nicely and might prove more convenient for my living family. Underneath this land that I ran above so many times, connected by taproot to Victoriana, in the city where poetry first entered my veins. The headstone, made of red granite, should read:

Chris McCabe (1977-)

Poet

Blessed on this earth with love

"I always fancied some time alone"

The playlist for the wake is included as an appendix to this book.

Machen's story ends with Arnold failing in his search to find Stoke Newington's paradise garden. He walks the (fictional) Canon's Park on his quest for it, but nothing unusual appears to him. He instead decides to go into a tavern to see if he can mine local knowledge for any further clues. Machen writes lovingly of Stoke Newington pubs, which then had the appeal of being 'outside London':

Arnold … beat the coverts of Stoke Newington, and dived into pubs of promising aspect, hoping to meet talkative old men, who might remember their fathers' stories and repeat them. He found a few, for though London has always been a place of restless, migratory tribes, and shifting populations; and now more than ever before; yet there still remains in many places, and above all in the remoter northern suburbs, an old fixed element, which can go back in memory sometimes for a hundred, even a hundred and fifty years. So in a venerable tavern—it would have been injurious and misleading to call it a pub—on the borders of Canon's Park he found an ancient circle that gathered nightly for an hour or two in a snug, if dingy, parlour.

Entering into a conversation with the locals, Arnold finds that Canon's Park has always put fear into the community, though nobody knows why. Then a man sitting in the corner tells them where the fear comes from: the park was the site of a 'lunatic asylum'. The story unfolds that one day a patient of the hospital escaped, and took up residence with a local landlady, whose suspicions begin to rise when the lodger began to talk of 'the amazing view you have from your windows'. As the house only looks onto other housing, with a small view of the urbanised Canon's Park, she asks him what he likes in particular:

"Everything"… he began to talk the most outrageous nonsense about golden and silver and purple flowers, and the bubbling well, and the walk that went under the trees right into the wood, and the fairy house on the hill; and I don't know what. He wanted Mrs Wilson to come to the window and look at it all. She was frightened, and took up her tray, and got out of the room as quick as she could".

The next day the 'madman' is taken back to the asylum.

I still say Abney Park Cemetery is Stoke Newington's paradise garden, just as Machen describes it in 'N'. What some people have described as madness can just as easily be explained as poetry. This was a tension in society that Machen clarified: 'So, I say, here is the problem: the common, widely accepted test of the right to existence of everything: does it pay, does it add to the physical comforts of life, is quite clearly opposed to the existence of poetry, and yet poetry exists. Therefore, either the poets and the lovers of poetry are mad, or else the common judgment is … let us say, mistaken.' Machen's garden, with its purple flowers, bubbling well (the culverted Hackney Brook) and the chapel – 'the fairy house on the hill' – describes this place I know and love; a place that I have discovered through poetry. My sense of smell has returned; I breathe in the arboretum.

As a final gesture to Machen, I find myself in The Jolly

Butchers on Stoke Newington High Street. I check my phone, which scrolls out news of potential variants to the virus, further restrictions, and the threat of another lockdown. I look through the window at the cemetery and imagine how it would feel to have access to London – and the buried garden – restricted again. I chase down the doom with a draught from my pint.

Then I look through the window and it is happening.

Noise and wild disorder at the cemetery gates. Above the gates, the clouds are swirling: a sepia mandala. I feel sprung, like a flea in the cream of a flat white. The poplars in the cemetery are spangling into Conder's ten-horned beast and the clouds have now morphed into angels, ringing out the trumpets of the Resurrection. Is that the Archangel, as prophesied in the cemetery's opening speech in 1840? The clouds are like ships, 'frigates of the sky'. A congregation of hack writers have gathered around the Egyptian pylons and a bird of prey soars over the lodge. A policewoman on a white horse trots past. I watch as an old woman appears from behind a headstone, frightening a small group of drunks who have been sharing from the same bottle. The wind picks up, turning the trees to rags. Red lightning and hail. I look at my feet and a large insect is scurrying into a hole in the pub floor, like a platelet forming on skin; it may be a cockroach, but my racing mind tells me it's a locust.

Expecting an audience of witnesses behind me, I turn to see couples lost in conversation and a lone man making small talk with the bar staff. People are emerging from hibernation; this moment is their new garden. I leave the last of my pint behind and cross the High Street, walking into mine.

The Garden of the Egyptian Dead, 2900 BC

O Abney-Anubis take me to your fields
Where the barley is more numerous than pollen
There my father walks in a violet light
We will retrace our steps through broken paths
And prepare our journey upwards
To the great silver disc of the skies
Which hovered above us all our days
Yes we can see the four columns
But what hope is there without your ladder

You my sky deity with the sun in your eyes

PLAYLIST FOR MY FUNERAL

'As the Beer Flows Over Me', Julian Cope

'Weird Fishes', Radiohead

'The Garden', Einstürzende Neubauten

'Pagan Poetry', Björk

'A Song from Under the Floorboards', Magazine

'It's the End of the World As We Know It (And I Feel Fine)', R.E.M.

'Oliver Twist (part 1)', Luke Haines

'Big Eyed Beans from Venus', Captain Beefheart

'Lost in Music', The Fall

ACKNOWLEDGEMENTS

I am hugely grateful to Arts Council England for awarding me Grants for the Arts funding to allow me to write this book.

As always, I am indebted to Tom Chivers for encouragement, insight and belief in this series of books. Thanks to Kate and Rosie at Penned in the Margins.

This book would not exist in its current form without the support of Abney Park Trust. Thanks to Zachariah Young, Trust Coordinator, for working with me at all stages of my research and to Haydn S. for helping me to find the graves of the poets with such extraordinary skill and attention to detail. Thanks to trustee Nick Toner for supporting this project. I would also like to thank Marina Szijarto, Alison Paler and other volunteers at the cemetery, for providing information on Alice Cron. Thanks to John Baldock for supporting this book in the first stages of its development.

Thanks to Jeff Johnson for background information on Iain Sinclair's writing.

Huge thanks to Iain Sinclair for walking with me in the grounds of the cemetery and opening up further avenues of thought relating to London's dead, poetry, Abney Park and Stoke Newington.

Thanks go to Caroline Ritchie for the spontaneous conversations about Abney Park, which began with William Blake and resulted in Caroline's poem 'Inter' being included in this book.

This book has been informed, shaped and improved by correspondence with the following people: James Byrne, Ste McCabe, Richard Price and Will René. Thanks to all for allowing me to quote their words.

And as always thanks to Sarah Crewe, the foundation of my garden.

SELECTED BIBLIOGRAPHY

Anonymous, *The Mabinogion*, edited by Jeffrey Ganz, London: Penguin, 2003.

Peter Ackroyd, *Poe: A Life Cut Short*, London: Vintage, 2009.

George Linnaeus Banks (editor), *Blondin: his life and performances*, London; New York: Routledge, Warne & Routledge, 1862.

George Linnaeus Banks, *Pearls from the Belfry*, London: Hope & Co, 1853.

George Linnaeus Banks, *Spring Gatherings: a collection of poems*, Liverpool: Whittaker and Co., and W. Grapel, 1845.

Isabella Varley Banks, *Ivy Leaves: a collection of poems*, London, 1844.

Isabella Varley Banks, *The Manchester Man*, Manchester: A. Heywood & Son, 1896.

Rev T.B. Barker, *Abney Park Cemetery: A Complete Descriptive Guide to this Beautiful Depository of the Dead*, London: Houlston & Wright, 1869.

Graham Beynon, *Isaac Watts: His Life and Thought*, Ross-shire: Christian Focus Publications, 2013.

Sue Black, *All That Remains: A Life in Death*, London: Transworld Publishers, 2019.

William Blake, *Blake's Poetry and Designs*, New York: W.W. Norton & Co., 2008.

William Blake, *Songs of Innocence and of Experience*, Oxford: Oxford University Press, 1989.

Robert Boyd, *Emily Gosse: A Life of Faith and Works*, Inverness: Olivert Books, 2004.

George Collison, *Cemetery Interment: containing a concise history of the modes of interment practised by the ancients; descriptions of Père la Chaise, the Eastern cemeteries and those of America; the English metropolitan and provincial cemeteries, and more particularly of the Abney Park cemetery at Stoke Newington, etc*, London: Longman & Co., 1840.

Josiah Conder, *The Choir and the Oratory; or Praise and Prayer*, London: Jackson & Walford, 1837.

Josiah Conder, *The Congregational Hymn Book*, London: Jackson & Walford, 1844.

Josiah Conder, *The Modern Traveller : A description, geographical, historical and topographical, of the various countries of the globe : Birmah, Siam and Anam*, London: James Duncan, 1830.

Josiah Conder, *On Protestant Nonconformity, Volume 1*, London: Joseph Conder, 1818.

Josiah Conder, *The Harmony of History with Prophecy: an exposition of the Apocalypse*, London: John Farquhar Shaw, 1849.

Josiah Conder, *The Star in the East; with other poems*, London : Taylor & Hessey, 1824.

S. Foster Damon, *A Blake Dictionary: The Ideas and Symbols of William Blake*, New Hampshire: Dartmouth College Press, 2013.

James Davis, *Eric Walrond: A Life in the Harlem Renaissance and the Transatlantic Caribbean*, New York: Columbia University Press, 2015.

Bernadine Evaristo, *Mr Loverman*, London: Penguin, 2013.

Paula R. Feldman and Daniel Robinson (eds), *A Century of Sonnets: The Romantic-Era Revival, 1750-1850*, Oxford: Oxford University Press,

1999.

Mark Fisher, *The Weird and the Eerie*, London: Repeater Books, 2016.

Charles F. Forshaw (ed.), *One Hundred of the Best Poems on the European War, by Women Poets of the Empire*, London: Elliot Stock, 1916.

James George Frazer, *The Golden Bough: A Study in Magic and Religion*, Edited with an Introduction and Notes by Robert Fraser, Oxford: Oxford University Press, 1994.

James Branwhite French, *Walks in Abney Park; with life-photographs of ministers and other public men whose names are found there ... With plan of the cemetery, etc. [Papers reprinted from the "Evangelical Magazine."]*, London: James Clarke & Co, 1883.

Edmund Gosse, *Father and Son: A Study of Two Temperaments*, edited with an Introduction by James Hepburn, London: Oxford University Press, 1974.

Emily Gosse, *Abraham and His Children: Or Parental Duties Illustrated by Scriptural Examples*, London, Bath [printed], 1855.

Emily Gosse, *Narrative Tracts*, London: Morgan and Chase, 1864.

Emily and Philip Gosse, *Sea-Side Pleasures*, London : S.P.C.K., 1861.

Philip Gosse, *The Aquarium: an unveiling of the wonders of the deep sea*, London, Bath: [s.n.], 1854.

Philip Gosse, *A Memorial of the Last Days on Earth of Emily Gosse, by her husband*, London : J. Nisbet & Co, 1857.

George Herbert, *A Selection of Poems by George Herbert, Chosen and introduced by Ruth Etchells*, Herts: Lion Publishing, 1988.

John Harris, *The Divine Rest: a discourse [on Heb. iv. 9] occasioned by the death of J. Conder ... To which is added the funeral address*, London: [s.n.], 1856.

William Hone, *The Political House That Jack Built (with thirteen cuts by George Cruikshank)*, thirty-third edition, London: Printed by and for William Hone, Ludgate Hill, 1819.

Edwin Paxton Hood, *Dream Land and Ghost Land: visits and wanderings there in the nineteenth century*, London: Partridge and Oakley, 1852.

Edwin Paxton Hood, *The Maid of Nuremberg, and other Voluntaries. [In verse.]*, Brighton: Privately Printed, 1873.

Edwin Paxton Hood, *Moral Manhood: in a series of orations, fables, and essays*, London: Patridge & Oakey, 1853.

Edwin Paxton Hood, *Sermons*, London, 1860.

Edwin Paxton Hood, *Swedenborg: A Biography and an Exposition*, London: Arthur Hall & Co, 1854.

Gerard Manley Hopkins, *Poems*, Oxford: Oxford University Press, 1970.

Alexander Japp, *Dramatic Pictures: English Rispetti, Sonnets and Other Verses*, London: Chatto & Windus, 1894.

Alexander Japp (writing as A.N. Mount Rose), *Facts and Fancies: from the Koran, the Doctors, etc*, London: T. Burleigh, 1899.

Alexander Japp, *Hours in my Garden, and other nature-sketches*, London: J. Hogg, 1894.

Alexander Japp, *Our Common Cuckoo and other cuckoos and parasitical birds*, London: T. Burleigh, 1899.

Alexander Japp, *Three Great Teachers of Our Own Time: Being an Attempt to Deduce the Spirit and Purpose Animating Carlyle, Tennyson, and Ruskin*, London, 1865.

Paul Joyce, *A Guide to Abney Park Cemetery*, London: Abney Park Cemetery Trust, 1994.

John Keats, *The Complete Poems*, London: Penguin Books, 2003.

Paul Koudounaris, *The Empire of Death: A Culural History of Ossuaries and Charnel Houses*, London: Thames & Hudson, 2011.

Raymond Lister, *Edward Calvert*, London: HarperCollins, 1962.

Thomas Toke Lynch, *Among Transgressors: A Theological Tract*, London: W. Kent and Co, 1860.

Thomas Toke Lynch, *Essays on Some of the Forms of Literature*, London: Bungay printed, 1853.

Thomas Toke Lynch, *Memorials of Theophilus Trinal, Student*, London, 1853.

Thomas Toke Lynch, *The Mornington Lecture: Thursday Evening Addresses*, London: Elliot Stock, 1870.

Thomas Toke Lynch, *The Rivulet: A Contribution to Sacred Song*, 3rd edition, London: Longmans Green, Reader and Dyer, 1868.

Thomas Toke Lynch, *Songs Controversial by Silent Long*, London: William Freeman, 1865.

Arthur Machen, *The Autobiography of Arthur Machen: Far Off Things and Things Near and Far, with an introduction by Stewart Lee*, Leyburn, North Yorkshire: Tartarus Press, 2017.

Arthur Machen, *The Great God Pan and Other Horror Stories*, Oxford: Oxford University Press, 2019.

Arthur Machen, *The Hill of Dreams*, Cardigan: Parthian Books, 2020.

Arthur Machen, *The London Adventure, or, The Art of Wandering*, Leyburn, North Yorkshire: Tartarus Press, 2017.

Arthur Machen, *N*, London: [s.l.]: Snuggly Books, 2018.

Miles Martindale, *Methodism Defended, in a discourse delivered on laying the foundation stone of Albion Chapel*, Skeldergate, York: Spence & Durdekin, 1816.

Alfred H. Miles (ed), *The Sacred Poets of the Nineteenth Century*, London: Routledge, 1906.

Dr Hibbert Newton, *The Flight of the Apostate. A poem ... With thoughts on our present Pre-Millenial State*, London, 1849.

Dr Hibbert Newton, *The Vale of Tempe; and other poems*, Dublin: W. Curry, June and Co., 1830.

Charles Olson, *Call Me Ishmael: A Study of Melville*, London: Jonathan Cape, 1967.

Wilfred Owen, *The Poems of Wilfred Owen* (edited by Jon Stallworthy), London: Chatto & Windus, 1993.

Edgar Allan Poe, *Eureka*, Surrey: Alma Books, 2018.

Edgar Allan Poe, *Tales of Mystery and Imagination*, Ware: Wordsworth Classics, 1993.

Caroline Ritchie, 'Inter', poem sent to author via email, 1st February, 2021.

Anna Shipton, *Tell Jesus: Recollections of Emily Gosse*, New York: Thomas Y. Cromwell & Company, [1867].

Iain Sinclair, *Back Garden Poems*, London: Albion Village Press, 1970.

Iain Sinclair, *The Birth Rug*, London: Albion Village Press, 1973.

Iain Sinclair, *Fifty Catacomb Saints*, London: Hoarse Commerce, 2018.

Iain Sinclair, *Kodak Mantra Diaries*, London: Albion Village Press, 1971.

Iain Sinclair, *Lud Heat: a book of the dead hamlets*, London: Albion Village Press, 1975.

Iain Sinclair, *Lights Out for the Territory: 9 Excursions in the Secret History of*

London, London: Granta Books, 1997.

Iain Sinclair, *Red Eye*, London: Test Centre, 2013.

Iain Sinclair, *Swimming to Heaven: the Lost Rivers of London*, London: The Swedenborg Society, 2013.

Iain Sinclair, *The Verbals: Kevin Jackson in Conversation with Iain Sinclair*, Tonbridge, Kent : Worple Press, 2003.

Sarah Stickney, *The Daughters of England, etc*, London, 1845.

Sarah Stickney, *The Island Queen: A Poem*, London, 1846.

John Stoughton, *Shades and Echoes of Old London*, London: Religious Tract Society, 1889.

Gina Luria Walker (ed), *The Idea of Being Free: A Mary Hays Reader*, Ontario: Broadview Editions, 2006.

Eric Walrond, *Tropic Death*, New York: Boni & Liveright, 2013.

Laurence Ward, *The London County Council Bomb Damage Maps 1939-1945*, London: Thames and Hudson, 2015.

Isaac Watts, *Divine Songs: attempted in easy language; for the use of children*, London: J. Buckland, 1780.

Isaac Watts, *Horæ Lyricæ. Poems, chiefly of the lyric kind; in three books*, [London]: Printed for W. Baynes, No. 54, Paternoster-Row, London, and C. Sutton, Nottingham, 1799.

Isaac Watts, *Hymns and Spiritual Songs: in three books*, London: printed for J. Bruce, D. Burnet, R. Hopper, R. Pennington and L. Martin, 1792.

Isaac Watts, *The World to Come: or discourses on the joys or sorrows of departed souls at death, and the glory or terror of the Resurrection, To which is affixed, an essay towards the proof of a separate state of souls after death*, Leeds:

Printed by Davies and Booth, 1817.

Ben Wilson, *The Laughter of Triumph: William Hone and the Fight for the Free Press*, London: Faber and Faber, 2005.

Mona Wilson, *The Life of William Blake,* London: Paladin, 1978.

ONLINE RESOURCES

Articles on Abney Park Cemetery found in The British Newspaper Archive, www.britishnewspaperarchive.co.uk.

Bethan Bell, 'Burial at sea: Seven things you might not know', BBC news, https://www.bbc.co.uk/news/uk-england-38210497 , last retrieved 19 July 2021.

Nicholas Casey, 'Rapper's Arrest Awakens Rage in Spanish Youth Chafing in Pandemic', New York Times, 27th February, 2021, https://www.nytimes.com/2021/02/27/world/europe/barcelona-protests-pablo-hasel.html , last retrieved, 29 June 2021.

Robin McKie, 'Did a coronavirus cause the pandemic that killed Queen Victoria's heir?', The Observer, https://www.theguardian.com/world/2020/may/31/did-a-coronavirus-cause-the-pandemic-that-killed-queen-victorias-heir, 31 May 2020.

Stephanie A. Mann, 'The Gorham Judgment, March 9, 1850', http://supremacyandsurvival.blogspot.com/2011/03/gorham-judgment-march-9-1850.html, last retrieved 22 Feb 2021.

Ellen Moody, 'Foremother Poet: Mary Hays (1760-1843)', https://reveriesunderthesignofausten.wordpress.com/2011/07/26/foremother-poet-mary-hays-1760-1843/ , last retrieved 12 April 2021.

Bridget Penney, 'our veteran tree walk', https://www.3ammagazine.com/3am/
our-veteran-tree-walk/ , last retrieved 31 March 2021.

Bridget Penney, 'think of this as a window: some graffiti and other
interventions at Abney Park Chapel, Stoke Newington, February 2007
to March 2010', http://www.3ammagazine.com/3am/think-of-this-as-a-
window/ , last retrieved 31 March 2021.

Kathy Rees, 'Edmund Gosse's Father and Son: Renegotiating Biography
Through Illustration', https://www2.le.ac.uk/offices/english-association/
publications/peer-english/peer-english-10/4%20Rees%20-%20
Edmund%20Gosse.pdf , last retrieved 4 March 2021.

Kathy Rees, 'The Graveyard Tract of Emily Gosse', The Gravestone Project,
http://thegravestoneproject.com/grave-notes/10982-2/ , last retrieved 23
March 2021.

Richard Smoley, 'Swedenborg's Apocalypse ... Now?', Swedenborg
Foundation, https://swedenborg.com/scholars-swedenborgs-apocalypse-
now/ , last retrieved 24 Feb 2021.

René Van Slooten, 'Edgar Allan Poe or Albert Einstein: Who was the
greatest thinker of all time?', Baltimore Post-Examiner, https://
baltimorepostexaminer.com/edgar-allan-poe-albert-einstein-greatest-
thinker-time/2013/12/28 , last retrieved 29 June 2021.

Chloe Wilson, 'Mary Hays: Author, Friend and All Round Radical', https://
eastendwomensmuseum.org/blog/2020/7/29/mary-hays-author-friend-
and-all-round-radical , last retrieved 12 April 2021.

All Poetry, 'Isabella Varley Banks, 1821-1897', https://allpoetry.com/Isabella-

Varley-Banks, last retrieved, 9 Feb 2021.

Conjubilant With Song, 'Thomas Toke Lynch', http://conjubilant.blogspot. com/2016/07/thomas-toke-lynch.html , last retrieved 31 March 2021.

National Fairground and Circus Archive, 'Frank Charles Bostock (1866-1912), https://www.sheffield.ac.uk/nfca/projects/frankbostockbio , last retrieved, 25 Feb 2021.

Our Migration Story, 'Germanophobia and World War 1', https://www. ourmigrationstory.org.uk/oms/germanophobia-and-germans-in-britain-in-the-early-twentieth-century , last retrieved, 29 June 2021.

Science Museum Group, 'Banks, Isabella Varley, 1821-1897', https:// collection.sciencemuseumgroup.org.uk/people/ap7300/banks-isabella-varley, last retrieved, 9 Feb 2021.

UK Wells, 'Elizabeth Fry (1780-1845), Quaker Minister and Reformer', https://ukwells.org/revivalists/elizabeth-fry , last retrieved, 25 Feb 2021.

INDEX